CU00594789

PARTNERS
IN ONE NATION

A NEW VISION OF BRITAIN 2000

PARTNERS
IN ONE NATION

A NEW VISION OF BRITAIN 2000

presented by
DAVID STEEL

edited by
David Steel and Richard Holme

THE BODLEY HEAD
LONDON

British Library Cataloguing
in Publication Data
Partners in One Nation: A New Vision of Britain 2000
1. Great Britain—Social conditions—1945–
I. Steel, David, *1938 Mar. 31*–   II. Holme, Richard
303.4'941   HN385.5
ISBN 0-370-30875-1
ISBN 0-370-30882-4 Pbk

© David Steel and Richard Holme 1985
Printed in Great Britain for
The Bodley Head Ltd
30 Bedford Square, London WC1B 3RP
by The Bath Press, Bath
Set in 11/12 pt Garamond
by Wyvern Typesetting Ltd, Bristol
First published 1985

Contents

David Steel

Introduction

The aftermath of a general election is always a dispiriting period—for everyone except the victors! After the General Election in the summer of 1983 I took a somewhat over publicised and exaggerated 'sabbatical' for three months from the leadership of the Liberal Party. On my return I realised that in presenting a constructive alternative to Thatcherism, it would be essential for the Liberal Party and the Alliance to win the intellectual argument against the new Conservatism.

So in the winter of 1983 I decided that the time was opportune for me to concentrate on discussion in depth of our Liberal ideas and values in preparation for the future, rather than competing in the media stakes with the newly elected Neil Kinnock, or for that matter my colleague in the Alliance as the new leader of the SDP David Owen. Politicians are sometimes criticised justly for talking too much and thinking too little.

I approached Ralf Dahrendorf, then retiring as Director of the London School of Economics, whose recent Reith lectures, articles and books I had found so stimulating, to see whether he would join me in chairing a series of seminars, during 1984, exchanging ideas with a team of regular participants. The thought was that each member in turn would deliver a paper about the Britain they would like to see in the year 2000 A.D. and then be questioned by other members under my chairmanship. These seminars, held in a committee room of the House of Commons, were open to Liberal

Liberal M.P.s and peers and members of the Party's Standing (policy) Committee who attended from time to time.

Thereafter we adjourned to the private room of a nearby hostelry where under Ralf's provocative chairmanship the seminar team continued the discussion over dinner (for which we each paid our share!).

Out of this process has come this book. I accept full responsibility for the final version, though each cited author has redrafted his paper in the light of our discussions, and in the practical editing I have relied on the publishing experience of Richard Holme. Each author has accepted our editing. Only some of the papers have found their way into the book. Others may not have been as central for our overall theme as these, but their ideas have been freely purloined and adopted within these papers.

My choice of participants in the seminar was highly subjective. They were all people whose intellectual distinction in their own fields I had previously admired, some active Liberals, others within the small 'l' liberal ethos but not necessarily committed to the party.

They were, in alphabetical order:

John Alderson, former assistant Commissioner of the Metropolitan Police, former Chief Constable of Devon and Cornwall, Visiting Professor at the Centre for Police Studies, Strathclyde University, Liberal Parliamentary candidate in 1983.

Ralf Dahrendorf, former FDP minister in the Federal Republic of Germany, former European Commissioner, then concluding his term as Director of the London School of Economics and now Head of the Department of Social Science, University of Konstanz.

Derek (Lord) Ezra, former Chairman of the National Coal Board, former President of the British Institute of Management, Liberal life peer, Chairman of Associated Heating Services.

Sir Ronald Gardner-Thorpe, former Lord Mayor of London, Chancellor of the City University, former Liberal candidate and former Treasurer of the Liberal Party.

Richard Holme, Chairman of the Constitutional Reform Centre, former President of the Liberal Party and Liberal candidate, former director of several major publishing companies.

Patrick Keatley, Diplomatic Editor of the *Guardian*.

James Meade, former director of the Economic Section of the Cabinet Office, former Professor of Political Economy at Cambridge University, winner of the Nobel prize for Economics, 1977.

John McCarthy, former Governor of Wormwood Scrubs prison, now Assistant Director of Residential Services, Richmond Fellowship.

Trevor Phillips, former President of the National Union of Students and presenter of London Weekend's 'Black on Black' programme.

Nancy (Baroness) Seear, former President of the Liberal Party, now party leader in the House of Lords, former President of the Institute of Personnel Management and of the British Standards Institute.

We were not all equally assiduous in our attendance, but the average was high. I am deeply grateful to them all, for providing such a range of ideas on how we could improve our country in the remaining fifteen years of the millennium.

David Steel
1985

1

David Steel

Economic Recovery Through Partnership

Over the last twenty years Britain has continued to slide
down the international league table of prosperity. In terms
of per capita GDP we were eighth among the OECD
countries in 1960: today of the twenty-four countries, we
are in seventeenth position. There is common political
agreement as to the reason. 'We have not been competitive,'
successive ministers tell us. But there the agreement ends.
Conservative ministers blame reckless unions and high wage
demands, which price us out of business. Labour ministers
castigate the lack of investment in industry. Both points are
valid but both ignore the deeply destructive effect which our
uniquely divisive political system has on our industry.

The first damaging characteristic of our post-war politics
has been that comparatively small changes in public opinion
have led to violent switches in public policy of a kind not
experienced by the multi-party democracies of Europe or
the two-party democracy of the United States. The scale of
the damage is difficult to quantify, but let me give some
examples.

The British steel industry was nationalised by the Attlee
government. It was denationalised by the Churchill government. It was renationalised by the Wilson government.
Small bits were sold off to private enterprise by the Heath
government and other bits sold by the Thatcher government. At the end of all this political horseplay we have a steel
industry hopelessly uncompetitive, which is having to be
drastically cut down in size. The unions may be partly at

fault and the management may also be partly blamed, but above all it is political mismanagement which has ruined the industry. When it was in private hands no one would invest in it because of the threat of public takeover. When it was in public hands there was no long-term confidence or morale because of the threats of its dismemberment. It has been the way to ruin an industry rather than to run it successfully.

Or take prices and incomes policies. Tory and Labour governments have each come to power pledged against any such policy; they have immediately abolished whatever mechanism they found in place, and they have then repented at leisure and established new policies and machinery. As a result, no long-term policy on prices and incomes has gained acceptance in Britain. It has never really been tried. All we have had is a series of short-term measures of varying degrees of effectiveness which have been introduced by governments which are on the record as not believing in them. The economic cost of stop and start on prices and incomes policy has been incalculable.

Or take aid to industry. Most advanced democracies accept the need for some state investment agency to provide a strategic boost for their economies. In Britain we first set up the Industrial Reorganisation Corporation and then abolished it. The National Enterprise Board was created and subsequently destroyed. The Tories flex their muscles against such bodies while Labour seeks to use them to extend state control of the economy. There has been no agreement on their proper and continuous function, which Ronald Gardner-Thorpe has usefully defined as 'finance and encouragement'.

Of the volumes of waste created by alternating governments each expanding the public bureaucracy while the nation is less able to afford it, the setting up of the Land Commission in Newcastle one year and its abolition the next stands out as a particularly striking example of these roller-coaster politics.

Each government devotes much of its energy in its first

two years to undoing whatever its predecessor did. Nowadays the ink is scarcely dry on a major parliamentary Bill before Her Majesty's Opposition is publicly pledged to repeal it. Each swing of the political pendulum threatens to take the country on yet more violently diverse directions to left and right. Thus the present 'non-interventionist' Tory government, more dogmatic and more doctrinaire than any previous Tory government, encourages a more left-wing socialism than has been seen in any previous Labour government. The political see-saw crashes up and down ever more violently to the discomfort of the ordinary citizen.

It is not just that our minority two-party system dislocates the economy, but the parties themselves are so composed that they are incapable of promoting national unity of purpose or industrial concord. They are still fighting the class war of the 1920s and 1930s. The Labour Party is financed by and controlled by the trade-union movement while the Tory Party is financed by and less obviously controlled by the interests of wealth and big business. Each looks after its own when in government and is opposed by the 'other side' of our society as being a wicked conspiracy interested only in its own kind. Thus the TUC is regularly consulted by Labour governments on their policy and the CBI relatively cold-shouldered, whereas the Conservatives conduct dialogue with the CBI and the Institute of Directors, leaving the TUC out in the cold.

These class-based attitudes pervade our housing, health and education policies as well as—and most directly—our industry. Against this background it has been difficult to get a sane hearing for the Liberal third way of industrial partnership, still less for our new thinking on the need to link the concept of profit-sharing with incomes policy. Yet a policy of pulling together is surely worth trying in place of the policies of pulling apart which have manifestly failed. The days in which British politics could be described in Trevor Phillips's words as 'the exercise of authority over burgeoning economic success' have gone for good. We need new ideas.

The public money poured into British Leyland, for example, should have been conditional on a plant-by-plant profit-sharing scheme. The creation and just sharing of wealth is the only way to put Britain back on her feet. Yet what is economically necessary is politically impossible for our present system to deliver.

But the most obvious failure of successive British governments has been the failure to secure sustainable economic growth without inflation. Labour governments in their attempts to keep the engine racing have paid insufficient attention to the dangerous tendency of the engine to pull the vehicle on a reckless inflationary course, reaching at points an annual rate of inflation of over twenty per cent. Conservative administrations, in their battle against inflation, cut swathes into public *capital* spending and use the weapon of unemployment as the means to cool the engine down. In his constituency election address in 1974, the present Chancellor of the Exchequer, Nigel Lawson, openly advocated this course of allowing unemployment to rise.

A fruitless philosophical battle then rages between rival schools of economists and politicians over the heads of the public: which is the greater evil—inflation or unemployment? The underlying assumption is that a choice has to be made between the two. I reject that fundamental assumption. The alternative course is to accept that fuller employment can be achieved if excessive wage increases can be controlled through some civilised incomes policy or, as I prefer, incomes *strategy* consisting of a number of policies.

The only tentative proof I have to offer that such a course might succeed is the eighteen-month period of the Lib–Lab pact. From the spring of 1977 to the autumn of 1978 the monthly rate of inflation was reduced from twenty per cent to under nine per cent with only a modest 0.5 per cent increase in unemployment from 5.8 to 6.3 per cent—still less than half the 1985 level. At that time, under the external constraint of the International Monetary Fund and the internal political constraint of the agreement with the Liberal Party, the Labour government was able to secure acquiescence from the trade-union movement for a vigorous clamp-down on wage demands.

Of course the policy was pursued by a series of ad hoc arrangements—arm twisting by government departments in placing contracts here; talks with the TUC there. The whole policy rested on ramshackle foundations and lacked any comprehensive structure approved by parliament. It worked for a short time, but as I have recounted in my book *A House Divided*, uncertainty about the ability to sustain the pay policy was at the heart of our decision to end the Lib–Lab Agreement in October 1978. I was prepared to argue the case for a solid pay policy in the ensuing election.

In what must rank as his greatest misjudgment, Mr Callaghan as Prime Minister decided not to hold an election then but to hang on for better times which never came. We entered the winter of discontent; the pay policy was destroyed, and the government fell and was heavily defeated at the subsequent election in May 1979.

Since then inflation has successfully been brought down but at the cruel price of a real unemployment level of nearly four million of our fellow citizens. I find this policy wholly unacceptable. The great oil revenues which were never at the disposal of any previous government have been frittered away on the huge current spending costs of the dole queue while forward capital investment, whether in our infrastructure or our education, has been cut.

The social consequences of individual bitterness, division between North and South in our country, the rising crime wave, and some would say drug wave too, have to be added to the economic costs. As John Alderson says in Chapter 9: 'No consideration of the police and the social order can evade the connection with the economic state of the nation.'

But my biggest criticism of this policy is that it is self-defeating. The followers of the present economic policies never seem to realise that if the defeat of inflation is obtained only at the cost of high unemployment, then what will happen when we pull out of recession is that we shall return to the old wage-push inflation.

That is why I return to my solution of an incomes strategy. It should contain three elements:

First, a national forum of discussion between government, industry and trade unions on the general state of the economy, the extent to which general pay increases can be afforded, and the need to price labour back into jobs. The present government has not established such a forum. It has not even taken NEDO seriously. It has alienated the trade-union movement by authoritarian sanctions as at GCHQ, and it has decreed arbitrary pay limits in the public sector while denying the existence of a pay policy. Labour governments by contrast have the unions permanently in bed with them. There must be a happy medium. Breaking free from the Labour Party would be healthy for the unions too, allowing them to represent effectively the real interests of their members, whichever government is in power.

Second, there must be some permanent body independent of government to which difficult demands can be referred. We have had several short-lived organisations in the past. We need one that will survive.

Neither of these proposals, though necessary, is original, but it is my *third* proposition which is new. Liberals have long advocated employee participation in both the finance and running of industry. This advocacy has tended to take conventional forms. We were pleased during the Lib–Lab pact to secure a tax incentive for employee shareholding which proved so successful that it was extended by the present Conservative government; we have looked favourably on the European system of elected works councils; we have admired workers' co-operatives such as that at Mondragon in Spain. All of these are useful parts of a general move towards a climate of partnership in industry.

But until now we have not seen our concept of industrial

partnership as part of a fundamental economic philosophy distinct from that of socialism or free-market capitalism. For some years I have argued that this was what was required. I am grateful therefore to two distinguished academics for guiding us in this direction. The first is Professor James Meade, whose history of political tutelage included Hugh Gaitskell and whose thoughts appear in Chapter 2.

He has confronted 'stagflation'—the terrible combination of stagnation and inflation—in a series of essays over the last two years, drawing on his great experience as a government adviser. He puts the question: how can one ensure that, with unemployment, an increase in total money expenditure will lead to an increase in employment rather than increased wage rates and prices? He rejects on the one hand the free-for-all approach of an unrestrained slave-labour market and on the other the extension of rigid government controls and interaction over pay and price levels, i.e. both the extreme Conservative and Socialist viewpoints. He is primarily concerned about the division of our society into 'insiders' and 'outsiders', a theme which recurs constantly throughout this book.

Professor Meade has argued for a system of tribunals required to decide pay levels most likely to increase jobs and he has advocated a move away from traditional trade-union freedom to engage in industrial action and instead towards an extension of their rights to obtain impartial settlement of disputes. He couples this with proposals for an anti-inflation tax (propounded by Professor Richard Layard and embodied in the last election Alliance manifesto) to be levied on employees who exceed pay norm increases.

The object of course would be to create a stable and permanent pay strategy instead of the endless series of temporary incomes policies which the country has endured. The system would be administratively simplified by confining its application to large-scale employers.

What makes James Meade's thesis particularly attractive

is the arrival of a complementary set of proposals from a younger economist, Professor Martin Weitzman of the Massachusetts Institute of Technology. His book *The Share Economy: Conquering Stagflation* could have as profound an effect on future political thinking as the works of the Socialist economists or the Friedmanites. I explored these proposals with him further on his recent visit to the London School of Economics.

Here I enter a strong *caveat*. In my view politics over these last twenty years has become too much the servant of economics, and politicians the slaves of economists. Thus the present Prime Minister sticks rigidly to the pursuit of economic theories which clearly need political adaptation. I did not agree, for example, with Martin Weitzman's rather dismissive reference to worker co-operatives. Indeed there is evidence that such as the Meriden motorcycle firm and the *Scottish Daily News* both achieved levels of productivity and efficiency greatly in excess of what went before. Their specific problem was that there was no market for their particular products. The National Freight Consortium has made an amazing turn-round from loss to profit since it was sold to its employees. So has Tyneside Ship Repairers. It lost £41 millions of public money in seven years. When it was privatised the workers bought it. A year later it made a modest £250,000 profit, two thirds of which was shared out to the workers. Everybody simply worked harder, spurning old demarcation rules.

As a Liberal and a pluralist I believe in a panoply of diverse measures all of which contribute to the same end— the creation of a partnership society in Britain.

But the central part of my thesis is that we should move from a wage-orientated economy to a share-income economy. In other words that a substantial part of the average person's take-home pay should be expressed not as a regular wage but as a share of profit earned or value added in the company to which he or she has contributed.

As Martin Weitzman puts it, 'the war against stagflation

cannot be won at the lofty antiseptic plane of pure macro-economic management. Instead it must be fought out in the muddy trenches of fundamental microeconomic reform. What is most desperately needed is an improved framework of incentives to induce better output, employment and pricing decisions at the level of the firm.' What is required is a new system of reward, introduced by tax incentives, to tie a worker's pay more to an appropriate personal share in a firm's improved performance.

That will build in the right incentives to resist both unemployment and inflation. A share system, I would argue, has a built-in drive towards absorbing unemployed workers, increasing output and lowering prices, which does not cease until all available labour is fully employed. Martin Weitzman expresses the thesis as follows:

> 'Were just one firm alone to convert from a wage contract to an equivalent share contract (initially paying the same compensation), that firm would increase employment and output, lowering its price, lowering its revenue per worker, and decreasing the pay of each worker. But if all firms (or a significant number) convert to a share system, something like a balanced expansion of the economy would take place, with the increased demand from higher spending of newly employed workers feeding back to keep prices, revenues per worker, and labour remuneration more or less steady but with the economy automatically going toward a higher employment level.'

Of course there is a risk that extensive participation in decision-making together with profit-sharing developments could encourage firms to reduce employment opportunities. To counter this we could draw on Meade, who has suggested it would be necessary in a share-wage society to abandon strict adherence to the principle of equal pay for equal work. Thus new employees might be taken on without qualifying for the additional sharing rights until after a set period of employment. In an age of high unemployment a period of admittedly low-paid work leading to participation in profits is preferable to endless dawdling in a dole queue.

Weitzman argues that capitalism scores over socialism in producing a variety of goods for those who can afford them, and consumer freedom of choice. Where it is less successful is in maintaining full employment and securing fair income distribution. He continues:

> 'The current wage system of compensating labour is a perilous anachronism that needs to be replaced. For when a contractionary impulse hits, not only is the initial response of a wage economy to throw people out of work, but a wage system can deepen a recession, multiplying its adverse consequences until the economy is trapped in a vicious circle of persistent involuntary underutilisation of the major factors of production.'

When a steel plant shuts down, the unemployed steel-worker cannot buy a car, a radio or a home extension made by other workers elsewhere. A ripple spreads across the country and indeed the world, leaving in its wake further shut-downs. Unemployment becomes self-sustaining and stagflation a vicious circle, a deadly trap. The unemployed steel worker cannot afford his new BL car because British Leyland has ceased placing sufficient orders with the British Steel Corporation. BL isn't placing enough orders with BSC because the unemployed steelworker isn't buying a new Maestro.

A partnership society would increase potential prosperity for the average worker and produce more harmonious industrial relations. Already Japan, to some extent the

United States, and even the emerging economies of Taiwan and Korea can teach us much in this field.

The existing economic system creates fixed nominal compensation for a majority who have work but a raw deal for the minority without it. It divides the workforce into insiders and outsiders. A share system offers the prospect of fuller employment at more fluctuating rates of pay.

When I tried these new ideas out, some months ago, on a group of captains of industry in London, they objected that some profits might be purely windfall and have nothing to do with the efforts of the employees. But so what? At present shareholders exclusively enjoy such windfalls— why should they not share their good fortune with employees?

In the United States some fifteen per cent of major companies have some element of employee profit-sharing, but typically this amounts to only between five and ten per cent of the average employee's pay. Clearly their effect can be at best marginal.

Weitzman for the purposes of his advocacy illustrates the beneficial effects of his proposal on an assumption of one third paid wage, two thirds share of profit. I doubt whether this is politically feasible, at any rate in one jump from our present systems.

But we could begin by offering a lower rate of taxation on the share-element of wages up to one third of the total, advancing after some years of experience to one half. The only major American corporation with a scheme as radical as this is Lincoln Electric with 2,600 employees. They've had no redundancies since their scheme was introduced in 1951 and report far closer worker/management co-operation.

In the capitalist system these examples will continue to be nothing but occasional curiosities until a deliberate tax-incentive policy is introduced by government. The Conservatives pay lip service to wider share-*ownership* but in practice confine their rather limited measures to giving cheap shares to directors and managers. Share ownership for *all* employees would certainly be a step in the right direction, but what is proposed here is far more fundamental.

It could be the single most explosive economic reform to revitalise our economy, create jobs and weld the nation together again.

I sketch out these new proposals knowing full well that the political feasibility of basic economic reform depends not only on its obvious merits but on the urgency of the underlying problem and the extent to which it is acknowledged that the traditional approaches of successive British governments have failed. Stagflation is the outstanding economic and social problem of our time and unconventional new solutions are required for it.

Unfortunately I do not believe that either of our post-war governing parties is so constituted as to be able to introduce such a fundamental change.

2

J. E. Meade

Full Employment, Wage Restraint, and the Distribution of Income*

My thesis is a straightforward one. A basic task for the Alliance over the remaining years of this century will be to persuade the electorate of the need for a fundamental shift of attitudes and reform of institutions as regards the setting of money wages and prices and the distribution of income and wealth. If our society is to be efficient, compassionate and liberal, less emphasis must be put upon using prices, and in particular upon using the price of labour, as a major instrument for achieving a fair and acceptable distribution of income; more emphasis must be put upon the setting of prices so as to obtain a full and efficient use of resources, and in particular of labour; and more attention must be paid to measures other than price and wage setting in order to achieve a fair and acceptable distribution of income and property.

The recent experience of severe stagflation, that is to say, of economic stagnation combined with the threat of a runaway inflation, leads inevitably to this conclusion. In a persistent stagflationary situation all governments find themselves impaled on the horns of a dilemma. If they increase the demand for goods and services by means of Keynesian expansionary financial policies, they may reduce unemployment but at the risk of a renewed explosive

*This chapter is a revised version of the first T. H. Marshall Memorial Lecture given at the University of Southampton on 1st November 1983 and published in *The Journal of Social Policy*, June 1984.

inflation of prices; if they follow Mrs Thatcher and restrain money expenditures, they can hope, as she has done, to fight the inflation but at a cost of massive unemployment.

The development of the social policies, institutions and attitudes which lie at the root of this problem can be well illustrated by three outstanding features of the policies of the post-war Labour government of 1945, namely: full employment, the welfare state, and free collective bargaining.

The commitment of the government to the maintenance of full employment marked a revolution in political ideas. For a quarter of a century after 1945 unemployment was held down to a figure varying between one and three per cent, as compared with the inter-war range of between ten and twenty-five per cent. This most desirable and successful development had, however, the important side effect of encouraging the idea that, since it was the government's responsibility to maintain employment, little or no attention need be paid, when formulating and pressing wage claims, to any possible adverse effects of high wage costs upon the demand for labour and so upon the level of employment.

This attitude has undoubtedly been encouraged by the building of a humane Welfare State. It is not suggested that the structure is a perfect one, and indeed it will be argued later that, as a means for redistributing income, it needs much further development. Unemployment can still lead to real deprivation. But if the position of the unemployed in the 1930s is compared with the position today, the contrast is indeed striking. The grinding poverty and complete destitution of the 1930s no longer occurs. Such a change is a most desirable one; but it has an important side effect on existing wage-setting institutions. Anxieties about possible effects of wage claims on levels of employment are reduced; and there is less possibility of undercutting agreed rates of pay by a desperate search for work at any cost by the unemployed.

But with the introduction and development of policies for full employment and for social welfare, free collective bargaining between independent, highly organised bodies of employers and employees becomes a most inappropriate and dangerous method of setting rates of pay. So long as full employment was successfully maintained by Keynesian financial policies, workers were apt to formulate wage claims without much concern about their possible effects on employment, even though they might aim at standards of real pay which were over-ambitious in view of the real productivity of their work; employers did not resist such claims with great determination in view of the general belief that, in order to maintain full employment, the government would in one way or another ensure that money expenditures were sufficiently increased to cover any increased costs of production; prices were then raised to cover costs; as a result money wage claims were further increased to cover the consequential rise in the cost of living; and the explosive inflationary spiral was completed.

At this point Mrs Thatcher or some other determined person is elected to restrain demand so as to fight the inflation, instead of expanding demand in order to maintain employment. There follows a reduction in inflation at the cost of mass unemployment.

There are deep roots in history for our highly emotive reactions to any criticism of this inappropriate and disastrous system of wage setting by what is called *free collective* bargaining but which, in the light of the richness of the English language, may well be translated into *uncontrolled monopoly* bargaining. For the first two thirds of the nineteenth century the workers had in effect no representation in parliament. To fight for a rise in standards through fiscal or other measures of parliamentary legislation was ruled out. The only method of asserting a claim on the community's real income was by the industrial action of organised bodies of workers who, in response to exploitation by employers, would ensure by monopolistic counter-action that no one, even if unemployed, would offer to work at a lower rate of pay. It is possible greatly to admire and to sympathise with this heroic chapter of the struggle by the underdog for freedom to establish institutions for uncontrolled monopoly bargaining; but this should not be allowed to blind one to the deficiencies of the system in the totally different circumstances of today.

This does not imply that there is no proper place for trade-union organisation. Production must be conducted on a large enough scale to be efficient. This means that one employer or employing body employs many workers. In conditions of imperfect competition this opens the way for great inequality of bargaining power unless the many workers combine to confront the single employer with a single seller of labour. For this, if for no other reason, trade-union organisation has a positive role to play and simply to bash the unions is not the way to cope with the present predicament. However, the actions of trade unions must be subject to social restraint because the function—indeed the proper function—of a trade-union leader in bargaining with the employer is the limited one of attaining the best possible conditions for the employed members of his union whose interests he represents, without any special regard to the interests of outsiders.

During a period of economic recession such as that experienced in the last few years the result is moderation in wage claims. As the demand for the products of an enterprise falls, the jobs of those in employment are threatened; and wage claims by those who are not yet unemployed are restrained in fear that they will price themselves out of their existing jobs. But when recovery comes and the demand for the products of an enterprise is expanding, the existing workers in employment are faced with a choice. Should the greater expenditure on their products be taken out in the form of a higher wage for those in employment, or in the form of an expansion of the numbers employed at the current wage rate? There is a basic conflict of interest

16

between the monopolistically organised insiders, who are interested in wage rates that maximise their income, and the unorganised outsiders, whose interests lie in wage rates that expand employment opportunities. This is not necessarily an argument against collective or monopoly bargaining; but I am arguing that, as in the case of other monopolies, society does have a duty to ensure that the prices which are set tend to promote output and employment rather than to ensure high gains to privileged insiders.

So much for the statement of the thesis that a reform of wage-fixing arrangements is needed to put much more emphasis on setting a price for labour which enables outsiders to be absorbed into the fellowship of the employed. The emphasis must be shifted on to measures other than the setting of rates of pay for the purpose of attaining an acceptable distribution of income. This is already the country's basic economic problem; but it may well become even more acute before the century is out.

There is no doubt that the country is now entering a period of extremely rapid and basic technological change which will have a dramatic effect in increasing the productivity of labour. As it has been argued above that its troubles are due to wage claims which outstrip the workers' productivity, it may at first sight appear that a new industrial revolution which increases output per head must at least help to solve the problem.

This may be the outcome; but, alas, it is not at all certain. Consider an office or a factory with a given amount of capital equipment and a given number of workers both before and after the technical change. The capital equipment will take a new form: tapes, word processors, and computers instead of filing cabinets, typewriters, and leather-bound ledgers; and robots instead of conventional machine tools. Average output per unit of capital equipment and average output per unit of labour would both have risen in the same proportion as total output, if the total amounts of capital and of labour had remained unchanged. But in this case what would have happened to the relative importance at the margin of capital equipment and of labour? It is possible, though it is by no means certain, that the nature of the inventions is such as to make the new forms of capital equipment very close and very efficient substitutes for labour, in which case the office or factory would be able to produce its new output at a lower cost by dismissing many workers and replacing them with a small additional amount of capital equipment. In a free-enterprise regime in which labour became less productive at the margin relative to the capital equipment, workers would be dismissed and re-placed by the more productive equipment, unless the cost-price of labour (i.e. the wage rate) was lowered relative to the cost of employing capital equipment (i.e. the rate of return on capital funds), with a consequent shift of distribu-tion of income from earnings to income on property.

The ultimate repercussions throughout society of these technological developments are so pervasive and so compli-cated that it is not possible to forecast with any assurance how far these possible adverse effects upon the distribution of income are in fact going to materialise. But in so far as they do materialise, there will be two possible lines of response.

In the first place, the wage rate might be allowed to fall in relation to the return on capital equipment; this would reduce the cost of relatively labour-intensive products and processes; if this went far enough, such products and processes might be expanded at the expense of the more capital-intensive processes to the extent necessary to pro-vide full employment. In this case full employment would be maintained but at the expense of a very unequal distribu-tion of income. The ownership of property is much more concentrated than the ownership of the ability to work. A relative rise in the profits going to the few rich owners of the capital equipment and a relative fall in the wages of labour would, to take a childish example, be compatible with a full-employment society in which the rich owners of the robots employed a large number of poorly paid butlers and other servants.

A second, and with present institutional arrangements a more probable, outcome would be on the following lines. The workers in the various industries, seeing the average output per worker being immensely raised and seeing the greater part of this going to the profits of the owners of the capital equipment, would through trade union or similar action insist that the wage rate was raised at least in line with the rise in average productivity, so that the price of labour was not allowed to fall relatively to the yield on capital. In this case, if technological developments were of the labour-saving kind discussed above, it would not pay producers to employ as much labour as before with the available amount of capital equipment. There would be a limited amount of well paid, perhaps very highly paid, employment of a few persons to look after the robots; the rest of the labour-force would be unemployed—or possibly in a few cases acting as poorly paid butlers to the few highly paid workers who were in employment or to the not-quite-so-rich owners of the capital equipment. The problems of the conflict of interests in the labour market between the insiders and the outsiders would be intensified.

These two possible scenarios have been described in childishly stark and simple imagery. Things will not happen quite like that. But these two simple fables may serve to make clear the two sorts of development which might occur to some degree. Neither of them is at all attractive. Surely there must be a better way of organising society so that new technologies which could enable everyone to have a higher standard of living than before will not threaten to lead to either of these disastrous situations. An efficient, compassionate, and liberal answer would be to attempt to devise wage-setting institutions which would allow the real wage rate to fall to the extent necessary to provide employment opportunities to all who sought them, but to combine this with fiscal and other institutions which ensured that, directly or indirectly, everyone enjoyed a fair share of the profits earned on the robots, computers, and tapes, and indeed on property in general.

In these circumstances the setting of the real wage at a level low enough to provide employment opportunities to all who sought them does not, of course, imply that employment will be on as big a scale after the technological improvements as it was before them. The technological improvements would have greatly increased real income per head, and the proposed fiscal arrangements would have ensured that this was enjoyed by all workers. History demonstrates that as income per head grows, people take out a large part of their increased standards in the form of increased leisure—shorter hours, later entry into and earlier retirement from the labour market, longer holidays, and so on. The wage rate would have to be kept down only to the level needed to satisfy a much reduced demand for work opportunities. What would be needed would be the development of social and economic arrangements in which the reduced work and the increased leisure were shared and in which leisure meant something more than inactive, idle boredom.

So much for the nature of the problem, a problem with which the country is already confronted and which may well be accentuated before the century is out. There follows a brief catalogue under nine headings of the sort of changes in policies and institutions which might set society on a new course in the desired direction.

First, the whole armoury of Keynesian instruments for the management of demand—budgetary policies, monetary policies, and foreign-exchange policies—should be brought into play. But the object would be no longer to control expenditures so as to maintain full employment, but rather to keep the total money expenditures on the products of labour on a steady growth path of, say, five per cent per annum.

Second, this financial background would mean that producers were safeguarded against any wholesale financial collapse in the markets for their products. But on the other hand they would realise that they could not with impunity raise their selling prices, since the total money demand for their products as a whole would be constrained. This atmosphere should be reinforced by other measures to promote competition and to restrain the setting of monopolistic prices by producers. The free import of foreign competitors' products, the development of the existing arrangements for the control of business restrictive practices, of monopolistic arrangements, and of mergers, and where appropriate the control of selling prices all fall into this category of measures.

Third, these restraints on the power and the willingness of employers to raise the selling prices of their products would increase their resistance to excessive money wage claims. They should be accompanied by measures designed to restrain the formation of over-ambitious wage claims. As in the case of the employers so also in the case of employed, the knowledge that financial policies are designed to limit the total amount of money income available for redistribution may help to restrain wage claims. But more positive action will be needed. However, it is not suitable to apply to a trade union precisely the same measures against restrictive practices as are applied to the sellers of other services and products. Existing legislation against restrictive practices in business prohibits agreements among independent sellers to set minimum prices below which they will not sell. To apply this to the sale of a man's labour would be to outlaw all effective trade unionism, since it would prohibit individual workers from getting together to agree on a wage below which they would not sell their labour.

Existing monopolistic powers of a trade union can, however, be judged excessive in a number of ways. For example, objection may be taken to certain arrangements expressly designed to keep outsiders out of the market, such as pre-entry closed shop arrangements which directly limit entry to the occupation, and unnecessary apprenticeship requirements.

Fourth, arrangements of this kind to reduce the powers and the incentives of both employers and employed to raise the prices of their products and their services need to be supplemented by a more direct control over the process of uncontrolled monopoly bargaining. For this purpose it would be helpful if some central council, preferably made up of representatives of government, of employers, and of employees together with outside experts, could agree upon a norm for an acceptable average wage increase over the coming year. Such a norm would have to take into account (i) the rate of increase planned by the government for the total of money expenditures on the products of labour, (ii) any need to restore or restrain profit margins and (iii) the extent to which it was desirable in the interests of full employment to increase the numbers in work. On this basis a desirable 'norm' for the increase in the rate of money pay per employed worker could be agreed.

The civilised way to proceed would then be to develop a nationwide structure of tribunals to which an unsettled dispute about pay could be referred. The tribunal might be required to make its award either in terms of the employer's latest offer or in terms of the employees' latest claim, and always to opt for the employees' latest claim unless the employers could show both (i) that their offer would be more likely to promote production over the foreseeable future in the sector concerned and also (ii) that their offer did not fall below the norm or adjust existing relativities by more than specified limited amounts. Sanctions can be designed against those, employers or employees, who take industrial action against the terms of the award.*

Such a system could in principle be applied to all employments in the public as well as in the private sectors of the

*See J. E. Meade, *Stagflation, Vol. 1. Wage-Fixing*, Allen & Unwin, 1982, pp. 115–17, and 'Wage-Fixing Revisited', Occasional Paper 72, Institute of Economic Affairs, London 1985.

economy. In the public sector the government will have to indicate the demand for the service in question by revealing estimates for future expenditures in the relevant public sector; and the tribunal, in the light of the expected norm to be earned elsewhere, would have to judge the rates of pay needed to man up the public activity before deciding whether the employing agency had made a case which satisfied the two criteria mentioned above. Since the government could, if it thought fit, always take a dispute to the tribunal, the system could act as a restraint on excessive inflationary increases throughout the public service.

This would not, however, be true of all cases in the private sector, where an agreement between employer and employees in a successful enterprise not to go to the tribunal, but to share the high rate of sales receipts between themselves rather than to expand the intake of outsiders at a rate of reward nearer to the norm, would always be possible and indeed, in many cases, probable. Such unwelcome developments might be restrained if the tribunal system were combined with a tax on increases in pay which exceeded the 'norm' by some specified amount.

Fifth, there is however an even more radical way of dealing with the wage-fixing problem in the more competitive private sector of the economy. This is simply to get rid of wages by transforming the pay of workers into a share of the total value of the net output of the business in question. Reform in this direction covers a multitude of different arrangements, stretching from minor profit-sharing arrangements to full-scale labour-owned labour-managed co-operatives, which are suitable only for reasonably competitive private enterprises. It is not possible to cover this immense subject at all fully, but there is one aspect of it which it is useful to treat at some length because it is of special interest and importance for Liberal policy.

Straightforward profit-sharing arrangements deserve every encouragement. It is not merely that they give the workers a direct interest in cutting costs and in the efficient running of the concern; nor is it merely that they can improve attitudes and relationships by helping to break down the barriers between 'them' and 'us'. They have the additional virtue of giving the employers of labour a powerful incentive to expand output and employment. The larger the proportion of the employee's take-home pay which takes the form of a share in profit, the greater will be the incentive for the employer to offer more jobs to the unemployed. The point can be most easily made by considering the extreme case in which the workers receive the whole of their pay in the form of a share in the value of the firm's net output, receiving, say, eighty per cent of the firm's net product, leaving twenty per cent of the net product for owners of the business. The owners in such circumstances would have a clear incentive to take on more workers to produce and sell more output, provided the sale of the additional output would add anything however small to the firm's net receipts, twenty per cent of any additional revenue being added to their profit.*

Such a share economy would thus lead to a very desirable expansion in the demand for labour; but, alas, it could lead to a serious contraction in the incentives of enterprises to invest in new capital equipment, since no less than eighty per cent of any addition to the firm's net output which was due solely to the investment of capital funds in new equipment would automatically be paid to the workers and not to the owners of the new capital. A share economy run in the interests of the owners of the capital would thus be expansionary in so far as the employment of labour was concerned but contractionary in so far as capital investment was concerned.

The interests of the existing workers would be exactly the opposite to this. A firm that was run on share-economy

---

*I am greatly indebted to Professor Martin L. Weitzman of the Massachusetts Institute of Technology for ideas on this subject. In his book *The Share Economy: Conquering Stagflation* (Harvard University Press) he makes a strong case for this solution.

principles in the interests of the existing workers would be expansionary in so far as capital investment projects were concerned (since the workers would get their eighty per cent of any resulting addition to the firm's net output, however small it might be) but would have a contractionary bias in so far as the employment of labour was concerned (since the capitalists would be paid their twenty per cent of the proceeds from any additional output due solely to the employment of new workers and, moreover, the existing workers would not want the marginal return from the new workers' production to bring down the existing average earnings of the workers who were already in employment).

There would thus be a severe conflict of interest between owners and workers in management decisions about plans for capital investment and for the employment of labour. But a main object of a sharing system should be to reduce rather than to increase these conflicts in decision-making; indeed in the interests of reducing the division between 'them' the bosses and 'us' the workers it is desirable to find some way of combining harmoniously a sharing of the income produced by an efficient business with participation in decision-making about the investment and employment plans of the enterprise.

It should be possible to modify the share-economy proposals in such a way as to avoid this basic conflict.* Imagine a firm in which all partners, whether capitalists or workers, own share certificates distributed among them *pro rata* to the incomes which they were receiving from the firm before the change-over to the share system. Everyone now receives the same income as before but in the form of a dividend on his or her holding of share certificates rather than in the form of wage, salary, interest, rent, profit, etc. All share certificates receive the same rate of dividend and for all basic

---

*For a more detailed scheme for labour-capital partnerships of this kind see J. E. Meade, *Stagflation, Vol. 1. Wage-Fixing*, Allen & Unwin, 1982, pp. 133–6, and 'Wage-Fixing Revisited', Occasional Paper 72, Institute of Economic Affairs, London 1985.

decisions about investment and employment plans carry the same voting rights. Capital share certificates are just like ordinary shares and can be freely bought and sold in the market. Worker share certificates, on the other hand, are tied to the particular worker and are withdrawn when the worker leaves the employment of the firm.

A new investment project can then be financed by the issue of new additional capital share certificates. If the addition to the value of the firm's net product due to the capital extension is more than the dividend payable on the newly issued capital shares, there is a net surplus available to be paid out on all existing share certificates to both capitalists and workers. An investment decision which more than repays its cost will be attractive to both partners. Similarly, suppose a new worker is taken on by an issue of an additional number of worker share certificates which at the current rate of dividend is sufficient to attract him or her into the working partnership. If the addition to the firm's net product due to the work of the new partner is greater than the dividend payable on the newly issued share certificates, then once again all existing shareholders, whether capitalist or worker, will gain from the surplus of the new worker's product over the new worker's dividend receipts.

This solution is fundamentally very simple, but it relies on one basic condition, namely: that in a successful capital-labour partnership of this kind newly admitted workers must not necessarily expect to receive as large a share dividend as the existing working partners. A numerical example may help:

Income of existing workers	£300
Value of product of new worker	£200
Income of new worker in previous position	£100

The existing partners will all gain so long as the new partner is offered new share certificates which carry a dividend of less than the £200 which he or she will add to the value of the firm's net product and the new partner will gain if he or she is offered more than the £100 earned in the previous position. But if the new worker had to be offered as much as the £300 earned by the existing workers, there would be a loss equal to the excess of the new earnings of £300 over the new contribution of £200 to the value of the firm's net product, which would have to be borne by the existing partners.

To be expansionary the principle must be that new hands are offered enough to attract them into the partnership, but not necessarily as much as the old hands are already enjoying. The new hands must rely on the fact that in due course as the old hands retire and relinquish their large shareholdings the new hands will inherit the privileged position of old hands. In other words in conditions of imperfect competition expansion of existing firms may have to rely on outsiders being admitted by insiders on terms that are attractive to both parties, but which may imply that the outsiders are not paid the same rate for the job as the lucky insiders. The outsiders must rely on the prospect of a future in which they will in turn become privileged insiders.

Sixth, there are many other ways in which the ability of outsiders to challenge the insiders might be encouraged. Of great importance are adequate arrangements for training unemployed outsiders in the skills needed for the expanding occupations. Another is the need for the encouragement of geographic mobility from a depressed to an expanding locality; and such mobility could be promoted if the housing market were freed from the present controls which tend to tie families to their existing dwellings. The arguments against such a policy rest on the possible adverse effect on distribution. Some landlords might make large takings in rents; some occupiers might be impoverished by having to pay higher rents. As in the labour market so in the housing market it is essential to combine the freeing of the market with fiscal and other arrangements for the redistribution of incomes, arrangements which impose high levies on the rich, whatever the source of their riches, and grant generous support to the poor and needy, whatever the causes of their poverty and needs.

Seventh, for the effective and generous relief of poverty and needs in a society with otherwise free markets a reform and integration of social benefits and of personal allowances under the income tax is, as Liberals have long argued, essential. All family units would receive a generous social benefit which would replace both the personal allowances under the income tax and also the broad range of social benefits for sickness, unemployment, basic state pension, children and other dependants, single-parent families, housing costs and so on. The amount of the social benefit allotted in any particular case would thus depend upon the beneficiaries' age, marital status, housing costs, number and age of dependants, and any other relevant factors. But as each beneficiary received additional income from earnings or other sources, these additional receipts would be taxed at an exceptionally high rate until the whole of the social benefit had been recouped. Suppose that the exceptionally high rate of recoupment tax were eighty per cent. Then, in the case of a taxpayer whose social dividend was set at £72, the first £90 of his earnings or other receipt of income would be subject to this eighty per cent rate of tax which would raise the revenue of £72 (i.e. 80% of £90) needed to recoup the whole of the social benefit, any income over and above this £90 being taxable at a lower basic rate of tax.*

With the present system there is a wholly irrational and incomprehensible muddle of complicated rules for the payment of national insurance contributions, of income tax with its various tax allowances, and of various social benefits, some subject and others not subject to means tests which themselves vary from benefit to benefit, and some subject and some not subject to income tax. This results in many people getting help who do not need it, while many

*A system of this kind could be devised to meet the generality of cases, though there might well remain certain special welfare needs which would be best treated outside this general structure.

who do need it get inadequate or no help. The proposed reform would not merely constitute a great simplification which would be less costly to administer and more easily understood by the man and woman in the street; but in addition, the universal payment of the social benefit would ensure that all those in need received help, while the special recoupment tax would mean that the cost of state aid was confined to those at the bottom end of the income scale. But any arrangement which gives generous help to those in real need without leading to an unacceptably high rate of tax on those who are better off has two inevitable consequences.

In the first place, it will necessarily imply a high marginal rate of tax on those at the bottom end of the income scale, since help can be confined to the poor only in so far as it is taken away from the poor as they become richer. In the above example there would at the bottom of the income scale be a marginal rate of tax of some eighty per cent. However, everyone would be sure of keeping at least twenty per cent of any additional earnings; and the system would thus effectively avoid the worst anomalies of the present muddled arrangements which can lead to a marginal rate of tax of one hundred per cent or more.

In the second place, at present tax allowances and social benefits which are not subject to means tests result in many better-off persons receiving help from the state which they do not need. Confining help to those in real need, as the proposed system would do, would eliminate this element of unneeded support of the better off who would to this extent be the losers. However, the result of this saving would be a great relief to the state's purse which could be used in part to finance the more generous benefits to the poor and in part to mitigate the loss of benefits to the better off by keeping down the basic rate of tax, which would also have a general favourable effect upon economic incentives.

Eighth, beyond the first slice of earnings or other income taxed at an exceptionally high rate there would extend as at present a progressive direct tax system, starting at some moderate basic rate of tax and then leading to progressively higher rates of tax as the individual's taxable receipts rose. It is, however, suggested that the basis of this progressive tax should be the level, not of the tax payer's income, but of his or her expenditure.

Ninth, two major reforms of the taxation of wealth and of transfers of wealth should also be contemplated. In the first place, there might be a progressive annual tax on the ownership of any wealth over and above a given tax-exempt limit, though such a tax raises formidable problems concerning the valuation of accumulated pension rights which in present conditions represent a very important element of private wealth. But, secondly, there should in any case be an effective tax on transfers of wealth by way of gift *inter vivos* or of bequest on death; the present capital transfer is so riddled with allowances, exemptions, and special arrangements as to be basically ineffective. But the proposed tax would be levied not, as in theory at present, on the cumulative amount of the gifts or bequests made by any single benefactor but on the cumulative amount of the gifts or bequests received by any single beneficiary, so that transfers to individuals who had received little property would be tax-free while transfers to those who had already been enriched by gift or inheritance would be heavily taxed.

Once again it is not possible to go into details; but the general logic of such arrangements can be clearly stated. If the preceding analysis is correct, it is desirable by one means or another to ensure that income from property is more equally distributed, whether by direct or indirect means. There are broadly speaking two ways in which this result might show itself.

The first and direct method would be by taking steps to achieve a more equal distribution of the private ownership of property. If every citizen were a representative owner of property as well as a representative earner of wages, the fact that an efficient use of the price mechanism required a fall in the wage rate relative to the return on property would not effect the distribution of income as between individuals; everyone's property income would go up as their wage income went down.

The tax arrangements outlined above are designed to encourage a more equal distribution of the ownership of property. The replacement of income by expenditure as the base for direct tax, together with a progressive annual tax on the ownership of properties above a certain limit, would enable those with small properties to accumulate larger properties without any tax on the savings from which the property was accumulated, while an annual wealth tax would raise revenue but in a way which made it more difficult for further concentration of large properties. In addition, a progressive tax on the total amount of property received by an individual by way of gift or inheritance would give a tax incentive for donors to hand on their property to those who had not already received much, and would inhibit the continued concentration of property as bequests to the wealthy from the wealthy.

The second and indirect method of redistributing income from property is for the state to acquire the ownership of property and to use the income from the property so acquired to finance the payment of social benefits on more generous terms. The drastic method of transferring the ownership would be by means of a once-for-all capital levy at a progressive rate on all owners of wealth of all forms. An annual wealth tax and the taxation of gifts and bequests which have been suggested above are less dramatic means for raising revenue which would be paid largely out of private holdings of wealth, and which the state could use either to redeem national debt or to invest in various ways in other forms of income-yielding property. In the case of previous nationalisation schemes the purpose was to transfer the management of real assets (such as the railway system) from private to public hands but at the expense of full compensation to the previous owners, so that the state made little or no gain or even some net loss on income account after setting the cost of interest payments to the compensated owners against the profits earned by the nationalised concerns. What is now proposed is a quite different topsy-turvy kind of nationalisation. It is not to transfer management into public hands, but by means of the general taxation of wealth and of capital transfers, to redeem national debt or to acquire for the public the unencumbered rights to a share of profits in enterprise whose management could be left entirely in private hands. The budgetary reduction in interest on the national debt and/or the receipt of income from the state ownership of shares in private enterprise would provide for the government a lasting net revenue which could contribute towards the costs of a basic social benefit.

So much for the blueprint of a New Utopia. Success or failure in moving significantly in the desired direction over the coming decades rests upon far-reaching changes in political and social attitudes. Over the last decade there has been a hideous and wasteful rise in unemployment in spite of the continuing existence of many useful things which unemployed labour and other resources might have been employed to do; the pay-off has been the successful containment of a real threat of runaway inflation of money costs and prices. But can a better way be found by an alliance of political forces which combines a resolute and effective attack on the inflationary setting of money wages and prices with a compassionate programme for welfare and for a decent distribution of work, leisure, and income achieved by other constructive, co-operative, but liberal measures? In the end a prosperous and healthy society, by increasing the size of the national cake, will be to the direct advantage of the vast majority of citizens. But the immediate appeal will have to be in large measure to the decent feelings of decent men and women. For although there is now a large army of outsiders, it remains markedly smaller than the fellowship of insiders; and the task will be to persuade the insiders to accept arrangements whose ultimate and indirect effects will almost certainly be to their own advantage but whose immediate and apparent purpose is to allow the outsiders to come in from the cold.

3

Nancy Seear

The Future of Work

Work is none the less work if it also happens to be enjoyable. You don't have to hate it. But it is essentially an activity in which the worker engages not for its intrinsic delights, but because it provides a livelihood. The livelihood may result directly from the work, as for the primitive hunter or fisherman, or indirectly through the brilliant device of money. I do not want the rabbits I have shot. You do. Fortunately I no longer have to rely on barter, which would presumably land me with your not very welcome potatoes. Instead, for my rabbits I get the cash you earned by the sale of your potatoes, and with that precious cash I buy the items I most desire.

Apologies to the economists. But I labour the point partly because in some quarters the system of barter is acquiring a halo. It is seen to rid the exchange of produce of the commercial taint of money. A less praised, but perhaps more genuine, cause of its popularity is the extent to which it avoids the obligation of tax. A more significant reason for stressing the apparently obvious importance of the exchange of the produce of work as a means of sustaining livelihoods is the pointer it gives to the consumer and to the moral basis of work. My work, which I put into the common pot, is the basis of my claim on the product of your work. It may not be the only basis for that claim. It is one of the purposes of this chapter to assert that there are other important grounds for such a claim, but it has always been, and it remains, one very important element in the claim. If this is true, then the person who takes the fruits of my work in exchange for the fruits of his, has a right to be satisfied with what he is getting. My work is also an important part of my contribution to society. Today, it seems often to be suggested that the purpose of work is to provide employment, not the goods and services society needs and wants. The right to work is often interpreted as the right to a particular job whether or not anyone is in the least interested in the product. Yet it is surely true that if, for reasons of my own, I go and dig holes in the Sahara till I am skin and bone from the exertion, I shall have been extremely active, but since no one has the slightest desire for the product, neither economically nor ethically have I any claim to be paid.

But in attempting to define the meaning of work it is also important to recognise society's perception of it as well as the perception of the individual. From society's angle work is surely any activity which in fact provides goods or services needed. If work is viewed exclusively as the means of livelihood of the individual it limits the range of activities that can properly be classified as 'work'. Yet society needs, for example, the activities of voluntary helpers in the health service; of unpaid political workers; of school managers; of good neighbours. Any view of the future of work needs to include such activities within its scope.

What does the individual hope to get from work? First and foremost, survival, or in our society, the money to obtain and maintain an acceptable standard of living. What constitutes an acceptable standard of living is obviously highly subjective, but determined in part at least by the standards of the local community and the individual's peers. But work is not only the source of material benefits. It also provides security, status, the respect of one's fellows and self-respect as a contributing member of society. For the specially fortunate it can satisfy intellectual curiosity and can be a major means of personal fulfilment, though it is perhaps worth stressing that, taking the world as a whole, survival is still the major reason for work. Only a fraction of the world's population have much opportunity for the luxury of personal fulfilment.

Whether they like it or not, work, then, is of major if not of prime importance to the vast majority of people. So two questions must be faced. Is there going to be work available for those who want it and, if the answer is 'No', how can the satisfactions work gives be provided in other ways?

Before accepting unquestioningly the prevailing view that there will not in the future be enough work to go round it has to be asserted and re-asserted that this is still a very poor world. Millions of people in the world have never had and still do not have enough to eat, certainly not enough to keep them in full physical health; millions of babies die who would live if resources were available, and even among the rich countries of the world standards of housing, education, health, leisure, to name only a few of the unchallengeably desirable good things of life, are in short supply. The world is not running out of work which needs to be done, it is running out of the capacity to pay for it and the political will and skill to match supply to demand. That this is a hideously difficult problem I do not deny. But it is surely the perspective in which Liberals, of all people, should be looking at the problem of work.

This being the case, it follows that economic growth is essential. Redistribution cannot begin to meet existing human needs, and experience to date surely suggests that redistribution policies—even very modest policies—are more likely to succeed in times of economic growth than under conditions of stagnation or decline. This is not to deny that there are important factors limiting the practicability of growth. Non-renewable resources cannot be carelessly expended; dangers to the environment must be avoided; the risks of inflation as a consequence of over-rapid growth are real. Yet without growth there is no hope of relieving the world's poverty.

In considering the future of work and employment pros-

36

pects in the United Kingdom, a number of points need to be emphasised:

1. It is essential to think of long-term employment prospects and not to allow decisions to be taken in response to the clamour to meet immediate needs. Politically this is very difficult, especially perhaps for Liberals who cannot bear to pass by on the other side even if by so doing they could contribute to a far greater good in the longer run.

2. Competition will get more not less intense. More developing countries are becoming newly industrialised countries, and newly industrialised countries become increasingly competitive. Industrial leadership has passed to Japan, and the US and the OPEC countries have great influence on all important energy supplies.

3. The nature of work is changing, with far greater need for skills and competencies than in the past.

4. The way in which work is organised is altering rapidly and much of our thinking about the organisation of work, based on the mass-production system, is becoming irrelevant.

5. Flexibility and rapid response to change is the name of the game, but many of the excellent practices developed to provide protection and security make such responses hard, if not impossible, and by so doing undermine the very security they were established to protect.

6. The future for the unskilled, and for those with nothing to sell but time and physical strength, is bleak in the extreme. At the end of the 1970s in this country forty-four per cent of our school-leavers either became unemployed or went into work with no training, compared with nineteen per cent in France and nine per cent in Germany. The long-term unemployed are made up overwhelmingly of the unskilled. It is probable that there are youngsters leaving school today, with nothing to show for their time at school, who will never have regular work or a regular income other than state benefits until they reach retirement age. These are the people who

constitute the 'underclass' of Professor Dahrendorf's chapter. 7. Powerfully organised sectional interests representing both employers and employed frequently block necessary change and wield great political power. Hence the importance of a political group such as the Alliance, which is not beholden to any sectional interest.

So what should we do? If we fail to compete we will not be able to begin to meet the aspirations for improved standards of living that have for long been taken for granted. Even worse, it is hard to see how our present unimpressive minimum standards can be maintained. So compete we must, with our eyes firmly on at least the middle distance. This means recognising that many of our traditional industries and enterprises must contract or disappear and we must put far more into research and development at the European Community level, the national level and the level of the firm. And this requires profits and confidence and the policies that breed them.

We must also recognise that work will be organised in a way quite different from the traditional pattern. Regular hours of work will be less important, the completion of the task more important. High-cost capital and equipment must be used to the full, requiring work in so-called unsocial hours, but also offering opportunities for very great flexibility of working time. Opportunities to share jobs, and to work from home, will be greatly increased, and should be encouraged, not regarded as a tiresome deviation from the norm.

We must also do everything possible to enable many of the unskilled to acquire skills, remembering that with modern training methods old dogs can learn new tricks and that we have in the past wantonly wasted the abilities of hundreds of thousands of men and proportionately even more women. We must do everything in our power to reduce the number of youngsters who slide into the unskilled grades and so into the ranks of the long-term unemployed.

Our best hope is to build on success and, out of the added value so created, to find the money to pay for the wide range of both public and private services for which there is a great potential demand, but no cash to pay for them. Many services will remain labour-intensive and many of these jobs can absorb people who do not have and will not acquire skills.

But it would be fatal to fall into the trap of believing that the development of service industries can by itself solve our problems. A country as dependent as is the United Kingdom on imports of raw materials and food survives by success in export markets. This in the main means success in exporting manufactured goods not only in the new high-technology field but also in established industries which have identified new markets and have applied new technology to their manufacturing processes. Some service industries do, of course, also bring in foreign exchange.

Of recent years our oil has to some extent compensated for our failures in manufacturing, but it would be folly to rely for the future on this means of paying our way. The ability to expand services and to create jobs in the service sector is a desirable consequence of successful exporting: it is in no way a substitute for it.

If we succeed along these lines there can be good prospects for quite a high proportion of the population. But when all this has been done, we shall be left with a residue of people, mainly among the unskilled, who will not find work. We can not allow this underclass to become a permanent characteristic of our society.

Liberals have always campaigned for decent levels of pay at the bottom of the pay scale and have joined forces to campaign with such groups as the Low Pay Unit. Extremes of wealth and poverty are anathema to Liberals and have no place in the Liberal Society of 2000. But it is none the less true that some people have priced themselves out of jobs. If labour costs were lower more people would be in work. There is no doubt that the black economy flourishes not least because, by evading social security and other charges, unit labour costs are lower in the black economy than in the open labour market. The self-employed often survive, especially in the early days, on 'sweat equity' and what is termed 'self-exploitation'—taking far less than the so-called 'rate for the job'. It is perhaps worth remembering that this 'rate for the job' is nothing more and nothing less than the rate the union succeeded in getting management to agree in the last negotiating round.

There is no escaping the inevitability of job creation if we are to avoid the continuation of a permanent underclass. As the Alliance has consistently maintained, some job creation should be the result of necessary capital expenditure on infrastructure which would expand the construction industry, with openings for both skilled and unskilled. There should also be increased provision of the most vital services such as home helps. In addition to these publicly financed jobs we need to build on, to improve and to make permanent, the community projects and voluntary projects introduced by the Manpower Services Commission. These schemes, at their best, involve genuine collaboration between statutory and voluntary bodies, are deeply rooted in local communities, serve community needs and rally local support and even enthusiasm. Different in origin, but perhaps even more the product of local feeling are the community initiatives where groups of people come together to provide goods and services which they recognise are wanted by the local community. Such schemes with backing from local enterprises, from local authorities and from voluntary bodies provide services and work and give income to those involved. If there is a profit it goes back into the community. Again, the pay is not in the 'rate for the job' class, but this undercutting appears to be acceptable because it is the community and not the individual entrepreneur which benefits. Such schemes provide those involved with some income, with something to do, with a place in society, friendly contacts and self-respect. In short, they provide genuine work and the rewards, both financial and psychological, that flow from successful work. It has to be faced, however, that the financial rewards can be very low.

Liberals need to think hard about this. Is it low pay they object to—especially when the alternative is no pay at all? Or is it low incomes? Surely it is low incomes. It is extremes of riches and poverty, poverty in the midst of plenty, which so deeply offends. Liberals have already gone far in finding the missing piece in the jig-saw. It becomes increasingly clear that for the Liberal Society of the future, some form of minimum citizen income-tax credit—call it what you like—is not a marginal extra but the cornerstone on which we can build. The minimum income does not have to be at subsistence level if additions are paid for sickness, unemployment, old age, child benefit. But even a small assured income for each individual would mean that small scale self-employment, participation in a community project or a local community initiative would, together with the citizen income, provide an acceptable standard of living. In this way, and it seems in this way only, a very high percentage of the underclass could find a place in society and a sense of belonging.

4

Derek Ezra

The Problem of Industrial Growth

Rarely in Britain's industrial history has the problem of industrial growth been more complex than it is today. In the period of some two hundred years since the start of the Industrial Revolution there have been many changes in the pattern of growth. These have been due to technological developments, competitive pressures and economic cycles. But it is not often that these circumstances have coincided to the extent that they are doing at present.

The existing situation has been further complicated by government policy and North Sea oil. The policy of the present government is to seek to control inflation and reduce public expenditure by limits on the money supply and the Public Sector Borrowing Requirement, and to leave everything else in the economy to market forces. This has created severe perturbations which will be analysed later.

North Sea oil has provided a substantial additional flow of income both internally and externally. This has masked to some degree the financial (though not the social) impact of the government's policies. The risk for the future is that these revenues are likely to diminish as North Sea oil production shortly reaches its expected peak.

Before carrying further the analysis of the present situation it is worth examining industrial developments since 1945, because much of what happened in that period of nearly forty years has influenced today's position. The period divides fairly clearly into three phases. The first phase was that of post-war reconstruction which lasted from the end of the war until about 1957. It was, above all, the phase of the Marshall Plan, when the Americans, having come out of the war in relative strength, contributed very substantial resources to the recovery of Europe—an act of historic generosity.

Under the Marshall Plan the economies which were damaged most were those that gained most. The British economy had been relatively much less damaged than that of Germany, or of France, Belgium and Holland, where the war had been fought on the ground. These latter countries built up new industrial structures, while Britain tended to patch up old ones. In the immediate post-war period, virtually everything was in short supply. If there was an enterprise that worked and produced there was no difficulty in selling its output. There was no incentive to introduce change if there was an existing industrial base. That was one of the many reasons why, subsequently, Britain tended to lag behind the industrial development of neighbouring countries.

The next phase, which was one of expansion, lasted from 1957 to 1973. That was a period when oil from the Middle East began arriving in large quantities and at very low prices, to be refined in the new plants that had been built in Western Europe as a result of the post-war reconstruction programmes. Those oil supplies provided what appeared to be a virtually unlimited, convenient and cheap source of energy. As a result of that situation, an unexampled period of growth ensued. European economies had been substantially reconstructed during the previous period, and they expanded beyond expectation in the 1960s.

However, mainly because in Britain there had been less physical reconstruction, growth took place at a slower pace. While there was a German economic miracle, an Italian one, a French one, a Japanese one, the British miracle never quite occurred. Britain tended to lag behind. What was disturbing in that period was that major new technological developments tended to take place in other countries. The modern steel industry was launched in Britain in the nineteenth century with the Bessemer converter, but the big break-through in the mid-twentieth century with the oxygen converter originated in Austria, and was followed in Lux-embourg, Belgium and Germany, and only came later to Britain.

Another reason why Britain lagged behind its Continen-tal neighbours was that the opportunity to join the European Economic Community—which had been freely offered at the time of the Messina Conference in 1955—was not seized. There is no doubt that the dismantling of internal barriers which occurred during the 1960s among the six original members of the EEC enabled them to take very full advantage of the conditions of peace and plenty which were prevalent in Western Europe at that time. While Britain responded with the development of the European Free Trade Area (EFTA), this was nowhere near as large, close knit or dynamic as the EEC. Nonetheless, during this period the British economy expanded, like others, even if more slowly. There was a stable currency, relatively low inflation, moderate interest rates, full employment, growing markets at home and abroad, and improving living standards. These were indeed halcyon days.

This tranquillity was rudely shattered by the swingeing oil price increases, first in 1973/4 and again in 1979. These led to a massive outflow of money to the Middle East, which in turn created serious balance of payments problems for the oil importing countries. International currencies were dis-rupted and the Bretton Woods agreement came to an end. Worse still, major inflation set in, markets shrank and unemployment rose.

Thus started a third post-war phase which can best be described as the phase of uncertainty, following on the phases of reconstruction and growth. Europe is still going through this third phase.

The major upsets in the economies of Western Europe took time to develop after the initial oil price shock of 1973/

74. In fact, the worst symptoms only emerged after the second oil shock of 1979. Then was ushered in the worst period of recession since the last war. Just as Britain had not advanced as fast as others in the period of growth in the 1960s and early 1970s, so it seemed to suffer more than others in the difficult times of the late 1970s and 1980s. This requires some explanation.

Part of the explanation lies in the fact that industry in Britain had adjusted less in physical and technological terms than industry in the main competitor nations. But there were probably two other major factors, one relating to government and the other to trade unions.

Throughout the whole of the post-war period governments in Britain have tended to act on a short-term basis. This may have been exacerbated, as David Steel argues in Chapter 1, by the sharp changes in direction caused by our adversarial electoral system, and it has had some harmful effects on industrial growth. The prevailing feature of the 1950s and 1960s was the stop-go system. Governments reacted primarily to the balance of payments situation. They cut back when the economy became 'overheated' and there were deficits on external payments; and applied a stimulus in the reverse situation. Furthermore, in between the recurrent balance of payments crises governments applied the policy of 'fine tuning'. This was intended to avoid major difficulties, but in fact added to those difficulties. The chosen instrument of fine tuning was purchase tax. This was moved up or down without notice and created real problems particularly in the consumer durable industry, where sale of refrigerators, washing machines and the like could be stopped overnight as a result of major increases in the tax. Happily, a more stable VAT system has now been adopted, but much damage was done at that time. However, similar difficulties arise even now with, for example, the present government's changing policy on grants for house repair. The introduction of these grants stimulated the appropriate sector of the building industry to expand, while their reduction, within quite a short space of time, has led to problems of over-capacity.

So far as the trade-union influence on economic affairs in the post-war period is concerned, this has been through some major changes. There was an initial phase of positive co-operation with the Attlee government and its policies. In the coal industry for example, not only was a very clearly defined consultative procedure written into the Nationalisation Act of 1946, but the NCB and the unions agreed that all disputes would go to arbitration, which would be binding. The prospect of strike action was further diminished by the obligation for the union to call a national ballot in a dispute and for a two thirds majority to be necessary before industrial action could be taken. It was felt that these various conditions would render strike action most unlikely.

During the course of the 1960s the unions' attitude progressively moved away from this position. Arbitration began to be distrusted as a means of settling differences, and unofficial disputes increased in intensity. In 1969 Mrs Barbara Castle, a leading member of the then Labour government, put forward proposals, under the title of 'In Place of Strife', to deal with these issues. But the strong opposition of the trade unions to any legislative curbs on their freedom of action led to the rejection of these proposals in June of that year and, instead, a 'solemn and binding' agreement was entered into with the government to deal with the problem through voluntary means.

There followed a period in which union power, especially on the shop floor, increased and industrial peace in a wide range of enterprises was purchased at the expense of substantial wage settlements. The attempt which the Heath government made in the early 1970s to introduce legislation to limit union power was strongly opposed and culminated in the miners' strikes of 1972 and 1974.

At the start of the ensuing Labour government further high wage settlements took place, stimulating inflation and reducing the competitiveness of British products. There followed a period of incomes policy, which operated with some success until the 'winter of discontent' of 1978–79, which in turn led to the defeat of the Callaghan government on a vote of confidence in the spring of 1979.

It is worth taking stock at this stage because, with the election of the Thatcher government, a new phase in British politics opened up. This was all the more important as it was accompanied by the most severe world economic recession since the last war. In 1979 British industry was in a potentially weak position and in no way ready to face up to the difficulties ahead. There were three principal reasons for this. In the first place, British industry had been less innovative in the post-war period than its major overseas competitors. Secondly, successive governments' stop-go policies and fine-tuning had interfered with industrial development and investment. Thirdly, the increasing militancy of the unions from the latter 1960s onwards had exacted a high price in the form of reduced industrial competitiveness.

So it was that when the post-1979 recession came, British industry and the British economy as a whole suffered more than other major industrialised nations. This was exacerbated by government policy, which, for the first time since the 1930s, was deliberately deflationary in a recessionary period. The economic objectives set by the Thatcher government were to reduce inflation and public expenditure, and the chosen instrument was the control of money supply. The high interest rates that ensued created serious cash problems throughout industry at the very time that world markets were contracting. The consequent retrenchment primarily took the form of labour reduction, bearing in mind the relatively high cost of labour which had occurred in the preceding period.

There is little doubt that these policies would have led to a severe financial crisis had it not been for the adventitious benefit of North Sea oil and gas. These exceptional resources provided the Government with over £10 billion additional annual revenue during the early 1980s, and some £6 billion positive revenue on balance of payments. Thus the massive contraction of British industry which took place from 1979 onwards and the exceptional level of unemployment, which shows no sign of diminishing, could be absorbed without apparent financial disadvantage. Indeed, a further cushion has been provided by the government's privatisation policy, which, at its peak, could yield to the Treasury some £3 to 4 billion a year and another £2 billion on top of this through the sale of publicly-owned housing.

A situation has, therefore, been created where British industry, already relatively weak at the start of the post-1979 recession, was further seriously reduced in capacity by the government's deflationary policy; and the financial situation of the nation was only saved by the unscheduled benefits of North Sea Oil, and by the sale of public assets.

The government contend, with their strong belief in the forces of the market, that the relative decline in manufacturing industry will be corrected by a corresponding growth in the service sector and in high technology. But it is difficult to see how this will work out in practice. For as far ahead as can be seen Britain will remain a major market for manufactured goods, as indeed will other nations, whether industrialised or not. But whereas Britain's major competitors are renovating and, in certain sectors, expanding their industrial potential, the reverse is the case here.

The consequence of this trend is already plainly visible in the balance of payments, where in 1983 for the first time since the Industrial Revolution, Britain suffered a deficiency in its balance of payments in manufactured goods. Nor is this deficiency marginal—in 1983 it reached £2½ billion and has since grown to a rate of £4 billion.

So long as oil exports bring in a surplus of £6 billion, deficiencies, even of this sort, on manufactured goods trade, can be offset. Unfortunately the two trends are likely to be moving in opposite directions. Overseas earnings on oil (even assuming no major break in prices) are likely to diminish from 1986 onwards as North Sea production reaches its peak. At the same time the trend on manufactured goods looks as if it will worsen. Invisibles have for some years been showing a net contribution (after subtracting overseas expenditure mainly incurred by government and tourism) of some £2 to £3 billion, and it is difficult to see how this can be dramatically increased.

On present trends, therefore, the outcome is likely to be a structural balance of payments deficiency emerging in the latter part of the 1980s, accompanied by continued high unemployment and a reduced industrial potential. The gravity of such a prospect in both economic and political terms cannot be over emphasised. Projecting this situation to the end of the century could see Britain entering a vicious circle of heavy social expenditure on the one hand and increasing overseas payment deficiencies on the other. The only consequences of such a trend would be steadily declining living standards and steadily increasing protective measures to safeguard what was left of the national heritage. The disposable public assets would long since have been sold off, and the North Sea revenues would be in decline. The props which have safeguarded the situation so far would no longer be there.

If these daunting prospects are to be avoided, major changes in policy need to be introduced without delay. This is a crucial period, and what is now decided in the form of economic and industrial strategy could well have an impact until the year 2000. The fundamental change that is called for is a policy of industrial revival.

The slight improvement in the economy noticeable in the latter part of 1983 and in 1984 has arisen from a surge in consumer spending in addition to the rising level of North Sea oil earnings. In industrial terms this has meant an improvement in distribution and services and in the lighter end of industry, but not at the heavier end. In geographical terms the South-East has gained most, and the Midlands and the North least. The concentration of heavier industry in the

North and the Midlands has accentuated the difference between North and South—and, while the long-running coal strike of 1984/5 was due to a variety of factors, the division between North and South was a major influence. The emergence of two economies, one moving at a much much slower pace than the other, is precisely mirrored in the ideologies of the two adversarial parties. This bodes ill for the nation as it approaches the year 2000.

A major correction to this divergent trend can be brought about by widening the area of industrial recovery. Increases in consumer spending, which have been the symptom of economic recovery in Britain since the war, have led almost invariably to more imports of manufactured goods rather than to more home production. The problem is how to correct this without resorting to protectionism.

There is an opportunity to do this in the broad area described as the infrastructure. Public-sector investment in Britain in the basic infrastructure services of the road and railways, water supply and sewerage, and housing have been declining progressively for nearly a decade, and this has become more marked in the past five years. The result has been substantially to diminish the quality of these services. Attention to this has been drawn repeatedly, not only by professional civil engineering bodies, but also by wider organisations such as the Confederation of British Industry and the British Institute of Management. The consequence of a reduced standard of infrastructure has been to diminish the amenity of living for the individual and to impose additional burdens on industry.

These would be reasons enough for increased capital investment in the infrastructure. But there is another more important consideration. The great bulk of the work done on infrastructure projects is undertaken by the private sector, particularly in engineering and construction. Generally speaking, these are among enterprises that have suffered most in the recession (the construction firms that have done reasonably well are those with large overseas operations or mainly concentrated in the South-East). A major infrastructure investment programme would help to reactivate this basic sector throughout the country as a whole. The main contractors would, in the normal course of events, sub-contract a major proportion of the work and this would help to revive industrial activity still further. The important consequence of this process would be to provide a major stimulus at the heavier end of industry, thus helping to spread recovery, rather than for it to be concentrated at the lighter end and in the service sectors.

The argument advanced by the present government against this course of action is that the resources are not available within public spending limits and that to go beyond them would be inflationary. This is not necessarily so. Increased expenditure on needed infrastructure would increase the competitiveness of British industry by providing it with better services; it would generate a substantial number of extra jobs, thus reducing social charges in the form of unemployment benefits and increasing the tax yield to the Exchequer; above all, it would help to bridge the gap between North and South. The government's aim is to keep the Public Sector Borrowing Requirement to a level roughly equivalent to between 2 or 3 per cent of GNP. This is substantially below most other industrialised nations, who have at the same time kept their inflation low. An increase of say, £3 billion in infrastructure investment would still enable the PSBR to keep within practical limits by comparison with other countries (some of whom have a lower inflation rate) and provide a much needed injection of growth in the industrial sector as a whole.

A second course of action to stimulate industrial recovery on a wide ranging basis would be to ensure that new technologies were applied as effectively as possible to existing industrial sectors. The tendency has been to encourage new technology, particularly in the field of information, as a sector in itself. But its importance lies in the extent to which it can be used to stimulate innovation in industry as a whole.

The *Economist* recently drew attention to the way in which the American industrial recovery is being based more and more on the application of technology to the so-called 'smoke stack' industries. The *Economist* concluded: 'The question for Britain is not whether to spend £400 million on a fifth-generation computer project, but what can the micro-chip do for existing industries in Bolton and Bradford.'

A third course of action is to mount a major campaign of import substitution. One of the most serious weaknesses facing the British economy is the growing imbalance of trade in manufactured goods. The figures speak for themselves. In 1982 there was a positive balance of over £2 billion and it had been much higher in previous years. Indeed, apart from wartime, Britain had consistently earned a surplus on its trade in manufactures since the Industrial Revolution. But in 1983 this turned into a deficit of £2½ billion and in 1984 it was £4 billion. While exports have continued to rise, imports have risen much faster. The problem is essentially one of stemming the import tide without resorting to protectionism, which would be self-defeating.

A practical way of helping to achieve this is through the more effective application of what has become known as a 'positive' purchasing policy. This is for large-scale purchasers in the public and private sectors to use their power systematically to stimulate British suppliers to meet their requirements on a competitive basis.

This has many advantages. For a start it does not impinge upon any international obligations as the emphasis is on the supplies being competitive. Secondly, the closer relationship between purchaser and supplier, which this policy involves, is to mutual advantage as both can learn to understand each other's circumstances better. Thirdly, research and development resources can be operated in a complementary manner so as to make the best use of those available on each side. Fourthly, substantial regular markets at home can be created, which, in turn and fifthly, can provide a base for a strong export drive.

This policy requires more effort on the part of the purchaser and a greater response on the part of the supplier than is traditionally the case between the two parties. For the purchaser it means that he must not take no for an answer—a reversal of the normal situation—but keep prodding potential suppliers, and for the supplier it means a readiness to adapt and innovate to obtain the order.

The scope for reducing import penetration on a competitive basis through the use of the positive purchasing technique is substantial. Taking into account the combined purchasing power of government departments, local authorities, nationalised industries, and large private-sector firms in manufacturing and distribution, there is a total purchasing volume approaching £100 bn. An additional 4% of this purchasing power alone directed, on a competitive basis, to the home market could wipe out the current trade deficit on manufactured goods. This is a policy which can, if systematically and consistently applied, lead to much more competitiveness and innovation among home-based suppliers.

Finally, the trade-union factor in British industry is fundamental. Since the latter part of the 1960s and thus for nearly twenty years major confrontations and difficulties have arisen. Legislation, while it may be desirable to provide a broad framework, cannot give the complete answer. What is necessary is to influence the state of mind. A major impact could be made on the attitude of many unions if it were seen that a determined effort was being made to reactivate industry and provide improved job prospects. Additionally, there should be positive encouragement of participation and involvement of all those working within an enterprise. Again legislation cannot provide the answer, except through removing possible impediments to share ownership through options and co-partnership. What is needed, as argued elsewhere in this book, is a more determined encouragement of the spread of participative systems which so far only a limited number of firms have successfully introduced.

Britain's industrial problem can only be really understood by analysing the situation as it has evolved since the last war. In the thirty-year period up to the oil crisis of the mid 1970s British industry as a whole tended to lag behind that of major competitors because of inadequate innovative investment, changing government policies and growing union militancy. During the phase of economic disarray opened up by the oil crisis the situation was compounded through the application of a tight money supply policy which substantially reduced the scale and scope of British industry. This process was masked, in financial terms, by the large earnings from North Sea oil and the proceeds from the sale of public assets. Both these sources of additional revenue are short-term, and the fundamental weakness of the industrial situation, with the growing split between North and South, and the continuing high level of unemployment, could lead to severe economic and social crises in the next few years.

To avoid this situation, with its dangerous implications of increasing political confrontation, action needs to be taken now when the resources are still available to reactivate industry on a wide-ranging basis by providing a more effective stimulus than has been the case up-to-date. Greater investment in much needed infrastructure improvements, a determined drive to apply new technologies in existing industries rather than concentrate on building up a new technology sector in itself, the application of positive purchasing policies to stimulate British suppliers to compete more effectively, particularly through import substitution, and a determined programme to spread participation and generate involvement within industry, are some of the measures which now need to be applied.

What is at stake is nothing less than the sort of society that will exist in Britain at the turn of the century. By continuing to pursue the present course the country will face the serious prospect of structurally high levels of unemployment, reduced living standards and increased tensions. A major change of course is now required to prevent this from happening.

5

David Steel

What Kind of Country?

One of the most fundamental divisions in politics is between those who think there is no limit to successful greed and those who know that this small planet on which we live needs looking after. For too long industrial societies, both capitalist and communist, have behaved like spoiled children with a toy-box, playing briefly with the marvellous gifts of the earth then breaking them or throwing them away. Our so-called consumer society with its insatiable demands for the world's finite resources and its intolerable costs in pollution has cost us dearly. Oil-covered oceans, radioactive beaches, chemical-filled rivers and lakes, acid rain and dirt-laden air, disappearing forests and concrete-covered farmland, scarred countryside and disintegrating cities all bear witness to the costs of what is at best negligence and at worst reckless greed.

Already in Britain there are the first signs of pending ecological disasters. It is becoming increasingly evident that we must act decisively to protect our environment and conserve our heritage. The Liberal Party has always been at the cutting edge of green politics in Britain, but ecological ideas are now gaining support in other European countries as well.

There are two things that must be done initially: first, people must be convinced that international action is necessary to solve the problems that man has created on this small planet which is our shared habitat. 'Ecology in one country' can only be a beginning. It cannot be a satisfactory conclusion. We must work with other governments and peoples to conserve our environment. Second, we must show that a decent environment fit to pass on to our children and grandchildren does not have to be an alternative to employment and rational economic activity. The best does not have to be the enemy of the good. We can have a green and resourceful economy.

Environmental concerns are not peripheral to society and the economy but central, an organising centre of core values. This was recognised in the Third Action Plan of the EEC Commission:

> 'Environment policy is a rational policy which
> is at the heart of overall socio-economic
> policies. Protection of the environment—
> although essential in its own right—can also
> be seen as a major aspect of long-term
> economic policy. This has major implications
> for the planning of economic activities of all
> kinds. Concern for the environment must
> increasingly be integrated into the planning of
> all such activities—agriculture, energy,
> industry, transport, tourism. Programmes
> constructed around environmental investment
> projects will have a beneficial effect on
> productivity. In other words, economic
> potential is likely to be reinforced through
> investment in scarce environmental resources.'

The European Community is already leagues ahead of the British government in its concerns and action programmes: as on so many other issues, Britain is the laggard. It is nothing short of a scandal, for instance, that the British government is prepared to go on exporting its acid rain to Continental Europe, risking our woodlands and forests and those of our neighbours, because of the opposition of the Prime Minister to anything which might interfere with the short-term interests of the Central Electricity Generating Board.

Europe has been the cradle of one of the greatest civilisations the world has ever known. How fitting it would be if a Community, which is searching for a new identity and purpose, were to set itself the target of creating a 'Green Europe' by the year 2000: with clean air, rivers, lakes and seas; with vital rural communities in a countryside alive with wild life and plants, producing food for our needs in co-operation with nature rather than at its expense; with cities cleaned, restored and rebuilt on a human scale; with a balanced variety of transport, public and private; with new industries based on re-cycling and re-use of resources, energy-frugal and high quality in output. This is the 'Europe of the people' that the wise men in Brussels are searching for.

We should recognise the deep dissatisfaction with our existing patterns of life in Western industrial nations. There is a search which unites people of different backgrounds, occupations and nationalities for a more authentic and natural way of life. They believe in the words of the Liberal Party constitution that 'each generation is responsible for the fate of the Earth and the balance of nature'.

In Britain alone there are more than three million people who by their membership of green organisations of one sort and another have shown their concern for conservation and the environment. There are many millions more who want to see a shift in priorities, who are searching for a new paradigm. We must build a bridge between their concerns and the real economy of jobs.

At the end of 1984, Madame Cresson, the French Minister of Industrial Redeployment and External Trade, reported on a series of measures to promote 'eco-industry', that is, the provision of manufacture and services in the field of anti-pollution and other environmental protection equipment.

The French have already achieved annual sales of over £1,500 million in technology for an eco-market that was not even dreamed of ten years ago. What is more, the French government have assisted this process. In Germany 400,000 people, two per cent of the work force, are now employed on environmental protection.

The Liberal/SDP Alliance in Britain have similarly identified the new opportunities in environment and conservation as a major source of new employment and exports. I should like to see a strong drive by government and industry to raise standards and then to develop the commercial opportunities that higher standards might afford.

On a wider canvas too, I am convinced that plans for the regeneration of the economy 'from the bottom up' by encouraging local enterprise initiatives and agencies should encourage the growth of that sector of the economy which is likely to use local material for local markets in a more labour-intensive way.

The growth—no/growth debate should be put to bed. What we should be talking about is building a strong economy with more full-time and part-time jobs, which uses and re-uses resources wisely and which is environmentally benevolent. The new and emerging technology can potentially help in this process, by making smaller-scale manufacturing easier and distributing information more widely. We cannot and must not turn our back on poverty and unemployment. On the contrary, we must show how the 'Third Industrial Revolution' could open a new area of partnership and worthwhile occupation for every citizen.

I particularly believe we need a more sensible and ecological energy policy. In energy policy, as in all aspects of economic life, the key lies in the choice of appropriate technology. I do not believe that the most appropriate technology to provide for our energy future is the most expensive, most dangerous and the most centralised option available, nuclear fission. I do not rule out R & D and I believe it is possible that nuclear fusion may one day be of interest, but I also believe that the Tory government's sense of priorities in pursuing a massive and expensive expansion of nuclear power stations is quite wrong.

It distracts attention from the real task which is to reduce consumption of energy through a thorough-going programme of conservation in domestic use and in industry and a greater emphasis on public transport. Just as proper environmental policies could provide employment opportunities, so could the development of heat-conservation products and techniques, like insulation and heat-exchange pumps. With government leadership and incentives, there could be whole new industries with considerable export potential. Yet the Conservative government actually cut back on its pathetically small conservation programme and relied on putting energy prices up. This is short-sighted. Energy conservation, seriously and extensively implemented, could save us thousands of millions of pounds, prolong the life of our own coal, gas and oil and give us longer to come up with alternative renewable energy resources for the time when the world oil supply becomes scarce again. It would also improve the competitiveness of British products.

Here too, the government, which is prepared to spend over £1,500 million or more per nuclear power station, spends under £15 million per annum on research into alternative energy sources. We should stand this crazy system of priorities on its head. Work should start on large-scale projects using wave- and river-barrage power. We should extend district heating systems, use industrial waste heat and install refuse-burning plants. Wind power and solar power should be the subject of maximum investment and development, in concert with our European partners. All these schemes would provide substantial employment. Clean energy using more appropriate and human technology could be a very great prize for Britain in the twenty-first century. It is surely a better legacy to leave our grandchildren than radioactive waste with hundreds of years of dangerous life ahead of it.

I should like to see a comprehensive National Energy Plan published, setting out the options and targets for open public discussion. I fear that without it we shall not take a sufficiently wide or long view of our energy futures. This need is all the greater in the wake of the coal strike. Decent industrial relations will not be restored in that unhappy industry without a long-term approach to the extraction and depletion of this major national asset. I also suspect that without an Energy Plan decisions will continue to be made, as they have been by both Tory and Labour governments in the past, behind closed doors in a secret and corporatist way.

It is particularly important to break secrecy on environmental questions. The need for more light could not be greater than in the debate on the future of nuclear power. In four key areas, insufficient public information is the common crippling factor.

First, *confidence*. There is no doubt that over the last five years the incidents at Sellafield and the handling of high-level waste, together with continuing scientific arguments, have undermined public confidence in the nuclear industry. The reason Windscale is so important is that it stands at the centre of our current strategies for dealing with radioactive waste. The future of nuclear power in this country depends, among other factors, on there being public confidence that radioactive waste can and will be safely disposed of.

I believe that either the Royal Commission on Environmental Pollution or a reconstituted Commission on Energy and the Environment should be asked to report on the whole issue of radioactive waste disposal in view of the technical, economic and political developments since the Royal Commission's sixth Report in 1976.

Second, *cost*. In the technical debate on the relative cost of nuclear power, the cost of waste disposal has been discounted. That not only distorts the present competitive position of nuclear energy, deferring to future generations the substantial cost which will arise, but it clouds a crucial area of the debate.

Third, *conflict*. There is growing public opposition to proposals for the siting of radioactive waste. The row over the choice of the ICI mine at Billingham as a site for

61

intermediate level wastes provided the government with a salutary warning when their plans for high-level disposal became clearer.

Fourth, *control*. There is a widespread feeling that the nuclear industry is insufficiently controlled by government and too little touched by independent review. Indeed, the tenth Report on Environmental Pollution, casting its net over a wider range, had this to say:

> 'Secrecy—particularly the half-kept secret— fuels fear. In our visits and discussions we have noted instances where quite unnecessary concern has been caused by people's inability to obtain information on the nature of a discharge of waste material.'

And it continues:

> 'As the Second Report put it:
> "Since many industries are going to great trouble and expense to abate pollution, they do themselves a disservice by needless secrecy. We believe that public confidence in the concern these industries have for the environment would be strengthened if this needless cloak of secrecy were withdrawn."'

In the end, actions speak louder than words on all the environmental questions which matter so much in contemporary Britain, from rural transport to nuclear power, from animal welfare to lead in petrol. We need a government with commitment. The Royal Commission on Environmental Pollution has made over 300 recommendations for action to protect the environment, yet less than ten per cent of them have been implemented. It is now time that we established a department with a Minister, with clear responsibility for environmental protection and a budget to match. This might be a first step to putting green considerations at the centre of policy-making.

Our built environment is in particular need of urgent

attention. Bad housing is one of the greatest causes of human misery in Britain today. The scale of the problem is horrifying—over a million houses officially classified as 'unfit for human habitation' and 80,000 families officially recognised as homeless. Yet the government has cut the housing budget.

The moratorium on capital spending by local authorities has done untold damage, both to the country's housing stock and to employment in the construction industry. Together with the short-sighted imposition of VAT on housing alterations and the cruel cutback in Home Improvement Grants, it has led to demolition rather than conservation and to a serious decline in standards of human occupation, with all the attendant social consequences. At a time when we should be investing, we are cutting back.

More resources could and should be found as part of a general programme of government-led public investment, financed by a small increase in the PSBR. We should aim to make enough money available to fund a public house-building programme of 100,000 new homes a year and to raise the annual slum clearance target to 40,000 homes a year. A national investigation should be set up to look into the structural condition of system-built council estates. It makes no sense for the government to be paying four hundred thousand building workers to do nothing when there is so much necessary work for them to do.

We need partnership between central government and local government. We need partnership in the renewal of our inner cities between directors of local companies, employees, residents, community associations and local councils which could make huge progress in land use and rehabilitation projects. We need partnership in local housing co-operatives, between single people or childless couples and local authorities, to rehabilitate near derelict properties, such as in the 'homesteading' and similar schemes. The potential for partnership is immense. It needs imagination and flexibility.

The major environmental challenge lying ahead is to make our great industrial cities places that people want to live and work in again. The country *needs* more development of new housing and renewed infrastructure. The construction industry is geared up to provide it. But the industry needs positive encouragement backed up with financial inducements to rebuild existing communities in the cities rather than turning to the easier and more profitable alternative of the green fields in the countryside.

The damaging directions of the present government's policies towards greater laissez-faire in the land market are amply illustrated by their attempt to build up to fifteen new towns in the South-East, several of them in the Metropolitan Green Belt. They tried to say there is not enough land to develop in the cities. Land there is too expensive anyway, they claim. County Councils in the South-East must be persuaded to release green-field sites for housing and positively forced to by the Environment Secretary if necessary, they argue.

But land in the cities is not the constraint that the government and some housebuilders say it is. It is not often appreciated that, even up to a few years ago, 30,000 new houses were being built each year in London alone. In the private sector, that figure is now down to little more than 5,000, with public sector housing equally savaged. The reason is not shortages of land but the cutback in public-sector housing programmes. This same message is given by all the major metropolitan housing authorities outside London covering our largest cities—land availability for new housing is not a problem. The willingness of the private housebuilders to develop there is the issue.

In Liverpool during the years when the Liberals without a working majority struggled to govern the city, bold schemes were introduced involving such partnership. I was proud formally to open one of the biggest private low-cost housing schemes on city centre derelict land anywhere in Britain, the result of an unorthodox approach, and indeed I opened a second scheme, even more daring because it was a mixture of private housing with council flats, thus enabling young couples to start on the path of home ownership while having a 'granny flat' available in the same community. It took months for the city council to obtain Department of the Environment approval for such a novel partnership experiment. It has been a great success. Significantly, the new militant Labour rulers of Liverpool have abandoned all co-operative housing schemes in favour of a return to the perpetual serfdom of endless council housing.

What is needed now is the same positive vision for the planning systems that brought in the landmark town and country planning legislation in the 1940s, the Green Belt directives in the 1950s and Conservation Areas in the 1960s. Planning has always been about a positive framework for guiding new development to where it is most needed in community terms whilst safeguarding areas of open countryside for the public.

Recently, green belts have come to be seen as playing that important role: redirecting investment to the places where it is most needed—the ailing inner cities. Within the last year, this positive guiding function of green belts has been accepted and encouraged by senior Department of the Environment inspectors in Green Belt enquiries.

No vision of the kind of country we seek to live in could be complete without some reference to the future of our welfare state. Liberals glory in their major part in its founding, first in the period of the 1906 government with the introduction of old-age pensions and unemployment benefit, and second with the implementation by the Attlee government of William Beveridge's health and social welfare plans.

Unfortunately, Labour and Conservative administration of a Liberal plan has quietly ignored key aspects of it. Beveridge foresaw a partnership between public and private provisions, not competition between them. It was no part of his vision that dependence on state agencies would replace

the care of family, friends and neighbours. Likewise, he
warned against creating barriers to individual initiative in
the social security system. Yet what else is the poverty trap?

Ralf Dahrendorf and Richard Holme examine these issues
later, and as Dahrendorf puts it:

> 'The Social State involves of necessity the
> setting up of bureaucracies which fail to reach
> the very individual cases with which they are
> supposed to deal.'

It is surely significant that the greatest number of complaints about our health and welfare services come from the
populous urban areas of our country where the bureaucracies are largest. Yet even in my own constituency, composed
of relatively small towns and villages, I have time and again
come up against lack of sensible caring action on individual
cases because the housing authority is not the same as the
social work authority which in turn is different from the
health authority, all of which are separate from the cash-
giving national authority of the Department of Health and
Social Security. Endless time-consuming and expensive
'consultative' meetings between all or some of these are
therefore the result. Locally, Liberals have never accepted a
network of appointed health authorities divorced from the
elected local government.

Naturally, we have watched with dismay the growth of
one bureaucracy assessing people's income for the purpose
of collecting revenue for the government (the Inland
Revenue) while another assesses people's needs for the
purpose of distributing government money for people's
needs (the DHSS). James Meade highlights this on page 28.

The answer to this muddle lies in a tax credit or negative
income tax where one agency assesses both means and
needs, and collects or disburses accordingly. This used to be
thought impossible, but the introduction of computer-
based data should now make such a scheme feasible and

cost-effective. It would sweep away some forty different assorted benefits.

All personal tax allowances, housing allowances (regardless of whether the citizen is owner or tenant), disability benefits, student grants and so on would gradually be introduced into the scheme as credits. The individual would pay into the scheme until the point where his entitlement to credits exceeds his liability to tax, thereafter he would receive appropriate payments from the scheme.

In both health care and education, we believe that no one should be driven into the private sector because of inadequacies in the public sector, which is why we have opposed crude reductions in expenditure which can have only that precise effect. The Liberal Party Constitution commits us to create 'the positive conditions which will make a full and free life possible for all'. The last two words establish an unbridgeable gulf between us and the Thatcher approach.

What links together the various facets of the quality of life in Britain which I have been discussing, environment, housing and welfare, is the concept of a partnership between an enabling government and democratically-involved local communities. The task of Whitehall is to change its role from management to enablement, setting standards, providing funds and dispersing power to assist the communities of Britain to look after themselves and plan for their lives in the next century.

6

Ralf Dahrendorf

The New Social State:
a Liberal Perspective

Not all Liberals have found it easy to come to terms with the Welfare State. While citizenship rights are a traditional and central liberal concern, there have been many who have confined their interest to the legal and political aspects of such rights, equality before the law, universal suffrage, political liberties. Given formal opportunities—so it was believed—citizens have to fend for themselves. Just as the market requires no more than certain rules of the game for all players, so the social and political community need do no more than provide the possibility of participation in its processes.

In the last forty years, the limitations of this concept have come to be widely acknowledged. (Indeed in Britain, it is Liberals and 'cross-benchers' who have contributed greatly to this recognition.) If people cannot afford to make use of their opportunities, these remain empty promises. The possibility of participation has to be rendered real by social policies which enable people to make use of the promise of citizenship. What T. H. Marshall* called social citizenship rights have had to be added to the legal and political rights. Thus, the modern Welfare State has come about.

Putting the case in this way is to cast doubt on the very term, Welfare State. It has overtones which are unfortunately patronising, not to say paternalistic—

---

*T. H. Marshall: *Citizenship and Social Class* (Cambridge University Press, Cambridge 1951).

although of course, there is also the much more neutral concept of welfare used by welfare economists, who are simply talking about measurable life chances. To avoid any confusion with the Poor Law tradition, indeed with the whole concept of a decent social position as charity, as something generously granted by someone else, I prefer the term, Social State. The Social State provides real citizenship rights for all.

Terminology is not intended to minimise the issue: we are here talking about something which Liberals also have found it hard to cope with, redistribution. The concept is rather less than clear. Most socialists have the vision of taking money from one group and giving it to another, a mechanical notion which either lacks realism or destroys liberty. The Liberal equivalent has two related elements. No one must be allowed to amass instruments of power (whether political or economic) which enable him to deny others their citizenship rights. Everyone must be enabled to have at least a minimum status of decent living. There is, in other words, both a floor and a ceiling of civilised existence, and between them, they constitute the necessary conditions of citizenship rights for all. This seemingly philosophical position has consequences for systems of taxation, of health care and social security, educational opportunity and unemployment benefits, in other words, for the Social State.

In most advanced countries, the Social State is a result of the experience of the 1930s, and of the politics of the 1940s. (Liberals, to be sure, have not played a dominant, or indeed a very convincing, part in either.) The structure of the Social State varies enormously from country to country. Some, like Britain, have regarded health care as its corner stone, others education, or old age pensions.* Some have relied on government as a guarantor of rights, others have chosen

*The differences are enormous. Percentage of social expenditure for pensions: GB 42%, Fr. 46%, W. Ger. 54%; for health: GB 32%, Fr. 30%, W. Ger. 25%; social security: GB 17%, Fr. 9%, W. Ger. 4% (J. Alber: Zt./ .Soc. 12/2, April 1983).

insurance-based systems.* The boundary between public responsibility and private contributions has been drawn differently in different countries. But everywhere, at least in Europe, a system has emerged which gives the rights of citizens social substance. In many ways, this system is the response of open societies to the challenges of class conflict.

It is important to stress that this development is fundamentally desirable. Indeed it was a necessary element of a process which began with the great revolutions of the seventeenth and eighteenth centuries and has led to unprecedented life chances for unprecedented numbers.

And yet: history is never finished. More than that, yesterday's successes are at the root of tomorrow's problems. The Social State in particular has by now generated as many problems as it has solved. A number of these, related and yet independent, require special attention:

The Social State is expensive. More than that, it consists of measures of redistribution which in the nature of the case involve growing expenditure. It was an error to believe that its elements are one-off measures (as some thought when the National Health Service was introduced in Britain). One can always do more, especially in the field of health care. Modern technology, coupled with new discoveries in preventive medicine, community medicine etc., make health care an almost open-ended commitment. The same is true for education, as one moves away from a one-off notion towards continuing education with all its implications. A similar statement could be made about care for the elderly. In fact, all constituent parts of the Social State have built-in multipliers of expenditure, and no built-in limits. It is hard to argue that some communities should have scanners, or opportunities for radiation treatment, or heart-transplant facilities, and others not. At the same time, it is, as it were, intrinsically impossible to provide ever more expensive services for all. Painful as this is, limits of obligation by the

*Again, there are significant differences: State: GB 50%, Fr. 23%, W. Ger. 26%; insurance: GB 17%, Fr. 19%, W. Ger. 30% (J. Alber).

community have to be defined, boundaries have to be drawn.

This conclusion is underlined by contingent developments which could not necessarily be foreseen. Such developments have led to a major, and continuing, increase in the number of recipients of social services. Educational expansion and the reduction of the retiring age are but two contributing causes. Demographic trends have led to significant changes in the proportions of those who pay into the Social State and those who have a right to expect support. At the core of such trends lies the shrinking importance, indeed the diminishing availability of work in all advanced societies. This raises structural questions about a Social State which is work-based, indeed job-based; but such structural questions, too, are preceded by increasingly insuperable obstacles to the financing of the promises inherent in the Social State.

Economic developments aggravate the issue. In most countries, the creation of the Social State coincided with an extended period of economic growth. This in turn was the basis of growing public income and thus public expenditure. As growth became more tenuous in the 1970s, increases in public expenditure, notably expenditure for redistributive rather than investment purposes, became more difficult. This is not the place to enter into the growth debate—crucial though it is for the definition of Liberal policies—but it would seem safe to say that we are not at this time entering another period of massive economic growth. This in turn means that, far from looking forward to a further increase in public expenditure, we are facing a time in which this expenditure, whether directly or indirectly incurred by the state, will have to be curbed.* More and more governments discover, in fact, that they cannot do anything else before they have come to grips with the growing debt of the

---

*This is of course also true for employers' contributions at a time of low growth.

state. Even if one is prepared to take a slightly more relaxed view, it is clear that there are extraneous as well as intrinsic reasons for setting a limit to the cost of the Social State.

Furthermore, the Social State is built on a paradox of which Liberals in particular are acutely aware. The problems which it is intended to solve are always, and by definition, individual problems, but the instruments which it employs are equally by definition, general instruments. One can put this less kindly. The Social State involves of necessity the setting up of bureaucracies which fail to reach the very individual cases with which they are supposed to deal. There are extreme examples. Today, skilled nurses spend as much time on administration as on nursing. The same is increasingly true for teachers. Indeed, advancement in these and other serving professions involves moving out of service and into offices. This means that the true subject of the Social State, the needy individual, is faced not with caring helpers, nor with ready assistance, but with queues and forms and officials and often humiliating processes. Much of the frightening bureaucratisation of modern life— of what Max Weber called the 'iron cage of bondage'— is in fact the result of the Social State. It means that in important respects this state has become self-defeating.

One further point is that the kind of problem which the traditional Social State is intended to solve may not be tomorrow's problem at all. The traditional Social State is based on the assumptions of the work society. Not only is it financed by those who have work, but it is also geared to people who essentially want to be a part of the world employment. Education is preparation for employment; health is the ability to do a job; retirement is the well-deserved reward for a lifetime of hard work; unemployment benefits are intended to tide people over an accident, at any rate an unusual period. But what if the real problem becomes one of defining considerable groups out of official society? What if the work society is only a part of reality, and some five, perhaps ten per cent or more find themselves permanently outside it? What if people's motives are no longer predictable in the terms of the work society? There may well be a new social problem at which such questions hint, and it is one which shows a new brittleness of the common floor on which all citizens are supposed to stand. For minority youths in inner cities, the Beveridge Report, let alone the Robbins Report, is no longer relevant.

Before these observations are turned into proposals, or at any rate principles for action, one general observation is in place. The quandary of the Social State is in many ways the litmus paper of modern politics. There are those who believe that the solution lies in more of the same, that redistribution was not sufficiently effective; they would destroy our liberties and our prosperity if they had their way. There are those who now argue that the whole process of redistribution was wrong in the first place and has to be undone; they are destroying the gains of citizenship wherever they have their way. Between the new socialists and the new conservatives, there are the social democrats who believe that by tinkering with the system we can make it work for some time to come. In an immediate and fairly short-term sense they may well be right, but they have no answer to the underlying issues mentioned here. The new pragmatists are merely survival politicians, essentially about the past rather than about the future.

Having said this, one is bound to add that there is of course no patent medicine. Indeed, Liberals distrust patent medicines as a matter of principle. More than that, any list of approaches is bound to fall short of the magnitude of the problem. Still, the following principles may provide a beginning of a Liberal answer to the problems of the Social State:

1. Neither the intention—effective citizenship rights for all—nor the method—redistribution—of the traditional Social State was wrong. There will continue to be a need to have redistributive mechanisms, essentially of taxation, in order to enable governments to help those whose citizenship rights would remain an empty promise without such

help. In other words, a massive dismantling process of the Social State cannot be intended.

2. At the same time, a major simplification of the Social State is both necessary and desirable. Its objective is clear. It is to provide a minimum status of civilised existence for all, rather than to try and cater for every contingency by separate (yet inadequate) provisions. The objective involves a simplification of machinery as well as one of financing. A semi-automatic mechanism such as a negative income tax based on defined minimum income is clearly preferable.*

3. Inevitably, however, the line between public responsibility and private contribution will have to be redrawn. This is necessary in view of the expenditure problems indicated earlier. It is also justifiable in view of the fact that social benefits have generally increased at a time of rising real wages when in fact they could be said to have a compensatory character. Indeed, it is nonsense that many should get as much back from the state as they pay (minus the friction cost of bureaucracy, of course). As a general principle, people should be expected to pay for their needs themselves.

4. The question then is: where does this principle cease to apply? Clearly, those most in need and least able to help themselves should be helped first. However, this is bound to lead to controversial conclusions, notably with respect to health care. Every social security system has its sacred cows; in Britain this is the National Health Service. Perhaps such symbols must be respected. In reality, however, it is hard to see how the Social State in Britain can come right without a massive extension of private health care, and greater contributions by all to health cost.

5. Among those most in need in a new social condition are the young. Vocational training, re-training, community service schemes, youth opportunities of many kinds, require considerable expenditure. While loan schemes may well be an acceptable method to finance higher and further

*For some detail see Lady Seear's chapter.

education, the new social problem of the underclass involves straight redistributive measures.

6. However, these have to be coupled with a new relationship between public and private, and more important still, bureaucratic and decentralised agencies of social service. The replacement of public bureaucracies by community networks is in fact taking place already. The process deserves and requires massive support by those concerned about individual life chances. There is an important new literature about small social networks in the place of office-centred social service agencies.* In the end, activating small communities is the only effective way to make sure that no one falls through the net of civic participation. It is significant that the new Militant-Tendency Labour rulers of Liverpool have cut support to voluntary community organisations.

7. Support for small social networks is in part a matter of attitudes, in part one of funds. These need not be big. Self-help groups require the encouragement of modest means. Local authorities clearly have a function here; but so does the voluntary sector. No one should expect the voluntary sector simply to step in where the state has left; not only the order of magnitude of needs, but also the unattractiveness of the proposition will deter foundations and other charities. But the voluntary sector can help greatly in bringing about the necessary change in orientation, from centralised heteronomy to decentralised autonomy.†

8. Underneath all this, one major change of approach will be required. It concerns the role of work, and notably of traditional employment. Just as it no longer makes sense to relate education mainly to job requirements, or to conceive of retirement largely in relation to a lifetime of work, so the Social State has to be seen as more than an extension of the work society. This has practical consequences; no system of

*J. Strasser: *Grenzen des Sozialstaats?* (EVA, Frankfurt 1979).
†R. Dahrendorf: *The Voluntary Sector in a Changing Economic Climate* (Charities Aid Foundation 1983).

taxation based largely on income tax will be adequate any more. It also has less tangible consequences; as we cease to think of employment as the pivot of life, at least what economists call 'voluntary unemployment' acquires a different place, as does the 'unofficial economy', and so does many another expression of people's desire to find their own answers in this time of uncertainties.*

Why should such principles be called Liberal (even perhaps with a capital L)? For one thing, they are more than improvised responses to a new predicament, while avoiding ideology and dogmatism. For another thing, their guiding idea is that it is the individual who matters. Without denying the need for government action, indeed for redistribution, the approach sketched here in its barest outline advocates less government, less bureaucracy, more individual contribution, more decentralisation. To be sure, it is an approach for a world in which real incomes are no longer rising in any spectacular manner. But it is also based on the belief that liberty need not suffer in the great uncertainties of the end of this century.

---

*'Activity' takes the place of 'work': a subject at which I have at least hinted in my *On Britain* (BBC Publications, London 1983).

7

Richard Holme

Political Accountability and the Exercise of Power

The British may have pioneered constitutional democracy but, looking at our contemporary political system, it would be difficult to guess that this was the case.

The checks and balances, envisaged by John Locke and enshrined in the American constitution, are conspicuous by their absence. Instead, the single principle of parliamentary sovereignty has been elevated above all others and then subtly corrupted to justify the absolute power of the Executive. Neither Parliament, as legislature, nor the judiciary has much opportunity to peer behind the thick curtains of State and see what is going on, let alone pulling them back and letting the light shine in. Executive power is here described as 'the State' advisedly since the Continental description now seems to fit the case better than the misleading romanticism of 'the Crown in Parliament'.

The British State is centralised, and becoming more so, and it is secretive, protecting its administrators and fending off the public and its representatives. With the failure of the Devolution Bills, the introduction of ratecapping and the recent onslaught on the GLC and the Metropolitan Counties, the trend to consolidate all major powers in the hands of Whitehall has been accentuated. As for secrecy, it is no coincidence that governments of different political persuasions have all found it in their interests to wrap themselves in the cloak of the Official Secrets Act and resist the demands for Freedom of Information.

Developments in the House of Commons have, on the

whole, been in favour of the State. Fifty years ago Ramsay Muir pointed out the tendency to Cabinet dictatorship supported by the whipped docility of MPs who are themselves the product of rigid party organisations. Today even such small diversity of view as a Cabinet may represent can be quenched by a strong Prime Minister, as we have seen repeatedly during the Thatcher administration, and party organisations have, if anything, increased their grip on MPs.

Thus Leviathan is untamed, whether by the advocates of free markets or by the champions of collectivism. We have arrived at the condition characterised by Lord Hailsham as 'elective dictatorship'. Yet constitutions are not acts of God: they are made for man and can be reformed by man. This chapter is therefore based on the hopeful premise that constitutional reform is both necessary and possible.

Let us first consider why it is necessary to change and improve our public institutions. Some, after all, would say they have served us well. Others would argue, more plausibly perhaps, that any rupture of the delicate web of assumptions which sustains our weighty, if invisible, constitution could bring it crashing down, that the consensus is already too strained to permit questioning of fundamental power relationships.

Yet if the consensus is strained, may that not to some extent be the result of a system which encourages confrontation rather than negotiation between interests, classes and parties? The British political system is binary, allowing only two logical positions, 'For' or 'Against', the 'Ins' versus the 'Outs'. Hegelian antithesis is easy to achieve in Britain. What is becoming almost impossible is creative synthesis.

To some, of course, this antithesis is the essential object of political activity, to sharpen up the lines of the class war and to polarise public opinion. By no coincidence the 'confrontationists' are happy with our system and, at least on the left, want to push it even further down the slippery slope to 'party democracy' as an alternative to popular democracy.

The British constitution, like a neglected company with great assets but poor management, is ripe for takeover.

A 'cadre' party, organised and controlled by perhaps 10,000 activists, could control the selection of MPs and then turn them from representatives into delegates; could insist on party election of all ministers; could, under our electoral system, achieve majority control of the House of Commons without much more than one third of the votes cast; could thus gain control of the State; could operate in complete administrative secrecy; could abolish the Second Chamber; could pass whatever laws it chose regardless of their effect on personal rights; and could resist any attempt by the judiciary to question the legality of its acts. Paradoxically, the only slender protection from such a takeover would lie in our membership of the European Community and our treaty accession to the European Convention on Human Rights. These, however, could be abrogated by the 'sovereign Parliament'.

It must be emphasised that this 'scenario' is not far-fetched. Every element of it is supported by substantial interests in the Labour Party. The result would be democratic centralism, Eastern-European style, where party control would be complete. And all this in a country which does not even boast a legal status for, let alone rules for the proper conduct of, political parties.

Negative reasons for constitutional reform are important. As liberal thinkers from John Stuart Mill to Isaiah Berlin have emphasised, the avoidance of tyranny should be the prime object of our political arrangements. If the exercise of what Karl Popper has called 'unchecked sovereignty' by even a democratically-elected majority threatens liberty, how much more so must this be the case when the 'sovereign' is a dedicated minority with a blueprint to transform society to conform with its own ideology.

Some Conservatives have shown that they are aware of this problem, yet in the past six years they have found themselves unable to do anything to initiate constitutional reform, save for the welcome strengthening of parliamentary committees by Mr St John Stevas when he was Leader of the House. To the normal disinclination of all governments to open up their administration to awkward questions, has been added the hostility of the Prime Minister, herself a confrontationist, who is impatient with what she sees as an abstract conceptual discussion without relevance to the practical business of government.

It is perhaps a failure of those of us who have argued for basic constitutional reform that we have not made the connection between open institutions and effective government with sufficient strength. The advocates of 'strong' government attack political reforms because they fear the restraints which may be imposed upon them. These restraints, they argue, will delay or even impede swift and effective action by the Executive. Proportional Representation might lead to lengthy negotiations between parties; a reformed Second Chamber might obstruct the will of the Commons; a Bill of Rights, incorporating the European Convention, might lead to challenges from the courts; greater devolution of powers to local government might obstruct central government; freedom of information might give rise to awkward questions.

The first answer to these blunt assertions of power should always be 'cui bono'. Naturally any Executive will find rules irksome and negotiations time-consuming but the constitution is not for the benefit of the rulers. It is for the ruled.

Nevertheless the critics of reform will persist, pointing out the complexity of modern government, the need to make clear decisions and how imperative it is to provide a definite sense of direction to the people at large who, after all, are not very political. Surely, they maintain, it is enough for the citizenry to vote every few years and then let the government get on with the business of governing.

The implicit model of politics these arguments reveal is hierarchical and paternalist. In management terms it is 'top-down' rather than 'bottom-up'—and indeed the appropriate response to it may be managerial as much as judicial, for management has moved on in an interesting way from the simple quasi-military models of command structures which were once the norm of all organisational theory.

A modern enterprise is far more likely to distribute knowledge than to centralise it; to promote involvement and participation rather than to discourage it; to share power and decision-making rather than to monopolise it; and to decentralise responsibility rather than keeping it all at head office.

Modern technology, which distributes information easily, has encouraged these trends away from hierarchical and rigid management. Microchips are potent agents of the dispersion of power away from the centre to the periphery. Yet there have been other reasons for the gradual democratisation and humanisation of industry which have relevance for politics too.

Progress, on which society like enterprise depends, requires a process of perpetual trial and error. Monolithic organisations are more likely to make large errors and then to hush them up. Open and decentralised organisations also make mistakes, but in contrast both the errors and their results are more quickly visible and the flexibility to adjust is greater. A liberal society learns from experience in a way that a closed society cannot.

On the positive side too, people have been found to contribute more to any endeavour of which they are a sentient part than if they are treated as automata fit only to receive commands and obey them. Power, like the farmer's manure, is best spread.

One of the limitations of traditional liberal political philosophy is that it takes the concentration of power as given. Indeed, the foundations of the British constitution were dug deep in the debate over two questions: whence did the monarch acquire his power, from God, the sword or the people? And how and in what circumstances should an unjust monarch, or tyrant, be resisted?

These questions of legitimacy and liberty have lost none of relevance in a century of totalitarianism but the emphasis on 'sovereign power' implies that the only questions of politics are who shall hold it and how it shall be wielded. The possibility that a society in which power is dispersed and spread so that, like the parable of the talents, it can flourish and multiply in the lives of the ordinary people, seems novel even today in one of the most educated populations in the history of civilisation.

Britain may have been a constitutional innovator once, but it has now become strangely conservative in its political arrangements, which have not evolved to keep pace with the changes in society. Power is grasped nervously to the bosom of the Westminster and Whitehall establishment and the citizen is restricted in his rights and responsibilities, in his rights to choosing once every four or five years who shall exercise that power, and in his responsibilities to making the best choice. The British constitution maximises the power of the State but minimises the role of the citizen. Small wonder that party ideologists of the right and left have found our constitution fit to their purposes. They can exercise power in the name of the people in theory but to the triumph of dogma in practice. The only real constraint upon them has been the intrusion of intractable reality into their theoretical omnipotence.

The paradox is that these alternating 'elective dictator-ships', each seeking legitimacy from a manifesto drawn up by its activists, have proved conspicuously unsuccessful in providing effective government for Britain. Not only have the abrupt changes of direction between them, far exceeding any change in public opinion, hindered successful management of the economy, but the level of consent necessary for government to achieve its aims in a complex nation of sixty million has deteriorated as the social fabric has worn thinner.

Far from accepting that democracy is the enemy of efficiency, the advocates of far-reaching constitutional reform must make the case for good government; not centralised, secretive, authoritarian government but dispersed, open and democratic government, responsive to the citizen, plural in its approach and ready to adapt its policies in the light of experience. This sort of 'good' government is the real alternative to the 'strong' government offered by the ideologists—and the closer 'good' government in turn approaches to self-government the better it will be.

How widely is this view accepted? There is growing unease about the British constitution and a widening movement for reform. Repeated opinion polls show a majority for specific reforms like Freedom of Information or Proportional Representation. The end of the Butskellite consensus on socio-economic issues has led to a spate of constitutional analysis. Nevertheless the political priority assigned to questions of institutional structure is still low. This may partly be because the system has suited the main players reasonably well. Yet it may also be partly the result of a British pragmatism which is mistrustful of formal or written arrangements for what has always been thought to belong to the realm of shared and generally unspoken assumptions, those tacit understandings which, as a cynical observer once said, are often misunderstood.

But the age of an underlying consensus is over. Both main players are now prepared to prosecute their aims and policies to the limit in a struggle for power which uses and abuses the conventions of the constitution rather than accepting and respecting them.

Major constitutional change has often been the product of great convulsion and revolution. A new constitutional settlement for Britain, therefore, poses a problem for a reforming party of incremental change like the Alliance. What was possible after the Civil War, the French Revolution or the American War of Independence or indeed on the occasion of the post-war emergence of our former colonies from British rule, that is to start with a clean slate, is not possible for a peaceful Britain in the last decades of the twentieth century. Nor should it be necessary. The foundations and parts of our constitutional structure are sound. What is needed is to take the old house seriously, to rebuild and extend it, to redecorate and illuminate it and to make it the living home of a hopeful democracy again.

We should be prepared to spend the remaining years of this century on a step by step regeneration of the constitution, conceiving this more as a *process* which will gradually revitalise our institutions and political relationships rather than an *event* which will magically transform the polity.

The habits and attitudes of active participatory democracy will need to be gradually learned and re-learned after generations of secretive paternalism. It will not be easy, for the attitude known to psychologists as 'learned helplessness' has been well taught in Britain. Every citizen who rails about the 'authorities' or 'them' from a perspective of frustrated impotence rather than knowing how to act to remedy his grievance and take charge of his situation is an adept pupil of paternalism.

That is why the prospectus for constitutional reform must be as concerned with the local and the particular, the seedbeds of democracy, as with our national institutions. Responsibility and a sense of community, the values and attitudes which allow an autonomous individual to function as an effective member of the wider society and which are in truth the indispensable cement of social life, can only be learned on a small scale.

Just as conservatives sometimes have difficulty with the idea of liberty, so liberals too often seem to shrink from the concept of responsibility. Yet liberty without personal responsibility is mere licence, doomed because it denies the central fact of human existence that, by origin, language, inheritance and mutual dependence, we belong to an irredeemably social species.

This concept of reconciliation between the needs of autonomous individuals and the wider society of which they form a part is at the heart of democratic constitutions. The constitution might be described as the sum of those basic rules which govern our life together and which thus help to determine the nature and quality of social relationships including, crucially, the distribution and exercise of power. These rules are enshrined in institutions which protect, interpret and implement them.

It is therefore impossible to argue constitutional reform merely from narrow or mechanistic premises. Questions of social ends as well as legal means are intrinsic to the discussion. Each constitution is an expression of the ultimate values of the society it regulates. These ends may be negatively expressed in terms of avoidance of tyranny, as early Dutch and English philosophers thought they should be or, more positively, in the terms of 'life, liberty and the pursuit of happiness' as the premature utilitarians of the American Revolution conceived them but, however uncomfortable it may be to contemporary pragmatism, constitutional law must deal with fundamentals.

For any liberal, and for the great majority of British people, these fundamental values will first include liberty and justice, but there are other less judicial ideas which should also, albeit in a subordinate position, represent constitutional 'goods' worth looking out for and attempting to enhance in our proposals for constitutional reform.

In Britain our constitutional aims should include the following: *sharing and dispersing power*; *building strong communities*; *generating wider consent*; and *increasing our ability to learn from experience*. As will be shown, these aims are by no means mutually exclusive, which is not surprising since they represent aspects of the partnership society which puts emphasis on the *potential* of its citizens working together rather than on a particular ideological prescription of what is good for them. It is the enduring strength of liberalism that it recognises the intimate connection between form and substance in human lives, or, in biological terms, that it sees the connection between structure and function. The way people do things determines and expresses who they are.

Sharing and dispersing power is, as has been said already, a relatively novel idea in a centralised nation state. From the Tudors to the Fabians, the strengthening of power of the centre has been seen not just as promoting administrative efficiency but, more idealistically, as providing redress for grievances and inequalities of the locality. The Crown, and its successor the State, were the sledgehammer to break the hold of the feudal lords and bishops. Yet coexistent with that growing power, Parliament, as a check upon the Executive, always had, in however imperfect form, the role of representing the claims of the localities, the boroughs and the shires, which in turn had their own evolving local government institutions.

Today, the necessary tension between centre and periphery has almost disappeared. Modern communication and the extraordinary extent of State power, subject only to the formal and limited restraint by Parliament, focus the political process on London. To a degree incredible in countries with a federal constitution or even with strong regional government, national government proposes and disposes. Napoleon would be impressed by British centralisation in 1985, particularly since France itself is now beginning to let go of the tight reins on which it has held its regions and departments since the time of the Emperor.

The reverse is true in Britain. The Thatcher government, in an attempt to implement its policies of fiscal control, has been ready to reduce the attenuated powers of local government even further. The claim has been made by ministers that any power of local government is enjoyed wholly and solely at the pleasure of Westminster, delegated as it were from the centre. In a unitary state, it is averred, local government has no intrinsic legitimacy. This is a historically dubious proposition. What is more important, it is wrong psychologically.

Local government in a mature democracy, with an educated electorate, is capable of doing and deciding more— not less.

The simple test is that each decision should be made at the closest appropriate level to the people affected by it. Thus we should conceive of the whole process of government as building from the bottom upwards, with residual powers and decision being passed upwards from parish and neighbourhood council, to district council, to county or regional councils and ultimately to Westminster. Beyond Westminster lie supranational institutions, notably the European Community, as a more suitable level for certain responsibilities to be exercised than the nation state.

This model of government is fundamentally different, and from a democratic standpoint healthier, than the top-down conception in which Westminster and Whitehall graciously 'delegate' powers to subordinate levels of government. This is why the notion of 'Devolution' never greatly commended itself even to the majority of Scots who wanted a national Assembly. The real question should have been put the other way around: what residual powers should Scotland freely vest in a British Parliament?

David Steel said of the Scottish referendum: 'No scheme of devolution will ever win public enthusiasm unless it involves genuine decentralisation from Whitehall, genuine reduction in local government patterns to one tier, reasonable financial independence and responsibility, and an electoral system which avoids domination by any one party or region of the country. The previous devolution package failed on all these tests. Our people were not impressed by a proposal which appeared to *add* bureaucracy and expense to what we already had.'

In respect of national services, like health and education, the prospect of greater local autonomy sometimes causes apprehension. Some of this is just the habitual nervousness of bureaucrats, faced by untidy pluralism instead of neat uniformity, but some of the fears are the result of legitimate concern that students or patients in economically or culturally backward parts of the country will lose out.

This risk has both to be diminished and then to be offset by the benefits of closer community identification and involvement. Although we should be ready to introduce local taxes, on income and sales, to fund a greater proportion of local government expenditure than is the case at present, the national exchequer should undoubtedly include in its residual powers an element of redistribution of funds to ensure that the provision of health care and educational opportunity do not fall below agreed professional standards anywhere in the country. Those standards should not just be quantitative but qualitative, to provide a framework of excellence, which allows for local variety whilst ensuring adequate care and curriculum.

At the same time, if secondary schools and hospitals were the responsibility of district councils, belonging to the towns and communities in which they were based, the level of local commitment to their funds and facilities would be higher and voluntary support activity of all kinds would be more easily achieved. Similarly, if the police were more firmly rooted in the locality they serve, the relationships between police and public might be closer and the deterrence and detection of crime easier.

In considering what intermediate authority, geographically and politically, is appropriate between the national centre and the locality too much emphasis can be put on the Redcliffe-Maud principle of uniformity.

Liberals have long been committed to regional government but the prejudice of this author is against any over-mechanistic division of Britain into large new authorities, even if they are disguised in historic costume as Wessex or Mercia. Clearly Scotland, Wales and, it might be argued, Yorkshire or the North-East, have the requisite sense of distinctness and 'place' but in the shire counties from Derbyshire southwards and westwards, it is the county, the city and the district which commands people's loyalties.

It might well be that the metropolitan county, to be abolished by the government, forms a better intervening level, in terms of population size, between the district and Westminster than would artificially constructed mega-regions, including the Home Counties doughnut around London. This would argue for federal groups of shire counties also coming together particularly for economic planning purposes, e.g. Surrey, Sussex and Kent or East Anglia or Avon, Gloucestershire, Hereford and Worcester.

It is appropriate to consider economic powers in relation to political, for Britain's economy is as centralised and hostile to local initiative as its polity. Vigorous local government should play a lively part in prompting local enterprise agencies to take initiatives in order to stimulate new business and local employment. This requires powers to invest in pump-priming these agencies. Such investments would achieve stronger gearing if large companies and clearing banks also adopt a more federal approach, thus allowing their local branches and units a greater degree of autonomy to play their role as constructive local corporate citizens than they often have the chance to do at present. Every part of Britain could benefit from a regeneration of the economy which was rooted, as it is in Germany or the United States, in thriving local communities.

In matters of land-use and planning too, there is scope for greater democratic involvement. The preparation of County and District Structure Plans provides an ideal opportunity for local consultation, with meetings and presentations in every town, village and ward to promote understanding among local residents of what is planned for their area and to identify significant dissent from what is proposed. There are few issues which stimulate involvement more than people's immediate habitat, the shape it will take and the amenities it will offer. If people are to move on from paternalism, the first and most obvious step is by asserting greater control over their neighbourhoods. Local environmental initiatives to prompt either a referendum or a planning inquiry, or both, on major questions of development and land-use policy might well stimulate informed citizenship and produce a more acceptable and human environment.

This discussion of the decentralisation of power inevitably leads to the idea of *building stronger communities* to which it is intimately related. The proposition is simply stated: when people are entrusted with the responsibility for their community they will give it more in terms of interest, commitment and money than when it is administered by remote bureaucracies, funded by undifferentiated central tax revenue.

Thus Ralf Dahrendorf's 'community network' conceived as the replacement for the expensive anonymity of the Welfare State depends on a new contract with the citizen. If the health service were returned as far as possible to the control of the community, and welfare services, like home help and meals on wheels, run in parallel with them, it is likely that the locality would organise provision for the sick and the elderly better than the man in Whitehall or the unaccountable Area Health Authority. The balance between relatively inexpensive home care and vastly expensive institutional care might improve, the humanity and emotional comfort afforded to patients might be more manifest and the willingness of the citizens to contribute both in local taxes and voluntary donations to 'their' services might increase.

This argument needs careful testing and validation, for the concept of the universality of health care should not be put at risk. Greater local autonomy would need to be exercised in the context of the national standards and redistribution of resources described above.

Nevertheless, the prize for getting the basis of stronger community provision right could be of great value. People might prove to be willing to dip into their disposable income to help fund their community's amenities in a way they never would via the Exchequer. The quality of service delivered might improve as a result of informed local control and involvement. The army of bureaucrats entrenched in the Health Service would find it more difficult to justify their existence. The ease of professional teams working together in the community could be enhanced.

The contribution which local control and community involvement might make to the Health Service, as it might to so many other areas of our national life, points the way out of the Welfare State impasse of declining services and escalating costs. The Thatcher solution has been privatisation, to reduce national services to market commodities to be bought and sold in packets by those able to pay for them and those commercial enough to provide them. The Labour solution is traditional: to provide central funds on demand to a national service, reckless of increasing demand and diminishing resources.

The alternative concept of a partnership between professionals and the community they serve potentially represents a liberation of new resources: of enthusiasm, caring and funding. It would need to be based on a new constitutional contract which offered greater control and autonomy for the community in exchange for greater responsibility and involvement on its part in the effective delivery of services.

The low turn-out by voters in local elections is often argued to be a symptom of indifference. It might equally be a realistic assessment by the voters of the relative powerlessness of local authorities in matters which most concern them. If secondary schools, local enterprise and health care alone were to become a clear local responsibility it would be interesting to see the turn-out improving.

Yet the concept of power being exercised in a responsible community cannot stop short at the local district. The very lessons learned there need to be applied at the county level, or federal county group, or city regions, or, in the case of Scotland and Wales, national, level on such matters as transport, roads, economic planning and tertiary education.

This process of democratic renewal, of re-establishing the nexus between democratic rights and communal responsibility, leads ultimately to Parliament and it is there, in the house of democracy which has become the home of the State, that we have to grasp the need for the third of our constitutional desiderata, *generating wider consent*.

The simplistic version of the British constitution in which the Crown, or Executive, proposes and the Legislature, or Parliament, disposes has tended to mean that, with the rise of party government, the House of Commons has been relegated to being little more than a safety-valve in a closed system. The Civil Service is trained to think of the House and its questions as awkward hurdles to be jumped over on the steeplechase of administration. Ministers know that, as long as party discipline holds firm by the none too subtle exercise of patronage and pressure, their legislation is safe. In most normal circumstances Her Majesty's government can proceed safely, privately and unaccountably.

There are honourable exceptions: independent backbenchers who are not content to be rubber stamps; Select Committees made bold by hearing expert evidence and finding themselves in agreement across party lines against the Executive; a House of Lords which is capable of kicking over the traces to force the government to think again; and even on occasion an irresistible popular outcry which penetrates the muffled precincts of the Palace of Westminster. Yet these are exceptions to the rule of government by private deliberation and public imposition. The 'Catch 22' for all modern British governments has been that without popular consent and understanding their policies fail and that, at the same time, the very system which guarantees the passage of their policies into law precludes the possibility of generating consent and understanding.

At the heart of the problem lies an electoral system which may have been very effective in gearing-up a popular minority of votes into a parliamentary majority but equally has been completely ineffective in delivering a government with a majority of voters behind it. With the emergence of a three, or according to some Social Democrats, a four major party system, the misrepresentation of public opinion in Parliament has become even more grossly capricious than it was in the 1950s and 1960s. Voters are inadequately represented in the range of their opinions by the range of their MPs. This creates a distance between the electorate and its legislators.

At the same time, because the winner-take-all electoral system does not encourage parties to reach out for every last vote in every constituency but rather emphasises the need to hold 'safe seats', the parties are encouraged in their 'laager' mentalities, huddling close to their own kind and avoiding too much dialogue with the wider electorate. Ideological activist control, amplified in manifestos, deepens the divisions between parties and simplifies the problems of a complex modern society. The very process of politics is conceived to be intra-party, eliminating any prospect of dialogue or discussion with non-party members in favour of a crude and highly-coloured contest between competing ideologies once every five years. In the process excessive expectations are aroused and unrealistic promises made. The stage is then set for another unsuccessful act in the Parliamentary drama, in the face of growing hostility from an electoral audience which does not like or understand what it is forced to watch.

A change to a proportional representation (PR) election system would be an important step in reforming the political system as a whole: it would ensure fairness by giving every vote the same weight no matter where or for whom it was cast; it would enhance the voter's power of choice within and between parties and candidates and thus re-awaken interest in the process; and it would ensure that no parliamentary majority could be assembled without a majority of the voters behind it.

Majoritarian government, whether formed by one immensely popular party or by a coalition of parties, would inevitably be more consensual government. Indeed it could not be formed in the first place without politicians willing, either in the election or the subsequent negotiations, to build bridges across the class, regional and ideological gulf which has divided our country for too long.

This concept of government by negotiation rather than by confrontation takes us back to the House of Commons itself. That the Executive should 'negotiate' with the House of Commons, largely through the medium of expert and adequately staffed Committees is a relatively novel idea which has yet to win full acceptance in Whitehall. It must not only be accepted but pressed further so that, as in the West German Bundestag, MPs can be involved in pre-legislative activity of one sort or another. The House, through special Joint Committees, might be involved as legislator, patron and recipient of major public planning enquiries for instance.

By the same token, the composition and role of the Second Chamber should be such as to make it a countervailing power to the Commons, representing different values and interests in the legislative process. Its composition should cease to be hereditary, substituting a balance of life peers, chosen for their distinction, and elected peers, whose election should be based on the nations and regions again by PR but at a different frequency from the Commons. The new Second Chamber should be the guardian of the constitution: it should represent the sort of long-term policy review body suggested by Sir Douglas Wass in the unlikely form of a Standing Royal Commission; and it should take a special role in relation to the regions. Save in these respects, its powers should remain as presently constituted.

As part of this process of creating a more responsive political system, the political parties themselves, as arrogant and secretive as feudal barons, must become more like the democracy that Britain itself should be. At present they are not even legal persons as they proceed turn and turn around to take over the power of the State. Their constitutions should be democratic, their accounts should be published, their income should be declared and their conduct should be within the law.

Financial openness from the parties will help build pressure for reform of a system of political financing which, by making Labour entirely dependent on Trade Unions and the Conservatives largely dependent on companies, again helps to institutionalise the model of Britain as the battleground for confrontation and class conflict.

Finally, in this plea for democratic government to be conceived of as a process of negotiation, rather than the blunt exercise of power, there is the question of the relationship of Parliament to the judiciary. Many attacks on the courts, particularly from the left, centre upon the persons of the judges. Are they not authoritarian rather than libertarian, narrow rather than broad in their sympathies, overprotective of property and not defensive enough of people?

If they are some of these things some of the time, is it possible that part of the explanation lies in their gradual loss of their historic role as guardians of human rights against the arbitrary exercise of power? Lord Scarman has described the proper relationship of Parliament and judges as 'partnership' to protect the citizen from the abuse of power but also by the continuous protection of human rights, to make the government of the day bring forward more humane and considered legislation. The passage of a Bill of Rights, incorporating the European Convention on Human Rights, will put respect for the individual at the heart of the system—and as has been argued earlier, rights and responsibilities go together.

The fourth constitutional aim reformers should have in mind is that of *increasing our ability to learn from experience*. The biologist Jonas Salk has pointed out that organisms which cannot learn from experience and adapt their behaviour are doomed to extinction. If the same is true of whole societies, Britain must be a strong candidate for the biological dustbin.

Systems of project review are almost non-existent in Whitehall and Westminster. The Public Accounts Committee plays the role of auditor with some distinction but the real problems of public policy decisions are not basically those of book-keeping errors. They spring from the inability of the governmental and political system to analyse the implementation of policy, its effects and the conclusions to be drawn for future policy. This problem has become more acute as the rise of ideology has made it a betrayal of faith for politicians and civil servants to question the efficacy of public policies. Any system of government which neglects the future and ignores the past is likely to be defective. It makes of each successive administration an end-game without memory and without hope.

The organisation of ministries and Whitehall Departments on traditional vertical lines, competing for resources and priority, contributes to this myopia. But the fundamental cause of our inability to learn from experience is not organisational. It is rather the secrecy with which the whole of British administration is deeply imbued. If knowledge equates to power, the Official Secrets Act becomes identifiable as an attempt to protect power by preventing the dissemination of knowledge. Ministers and their civil servants can retreat at will behind its protection, concealing their acts and the consequences that spring from them.

Repeal of the catch-all Section 2 of the Official Secrets Act and the introduction of Freedom of Information are essential not to catch administrators out but to inform and educate the citizen so that he or she can understand and participate. If power is to be spread and dispersed, knowledge must be made readily available to all who can and would use it.

Ronald Levinson in his *Defense of Plato* described Karl Popper's conviction 'that the greatest of all revolutions is the transition from the "closed society" to the "open society", an association of free individuals respecting each other's rights within the framework of mutual protection supplied by the State, and achieving, through the making of responsible, rational decisions, a growing measure of humane and enlightened life.'

That revolution which started in these islands has yet to be consummated. Each of the features of the new constitutional settlement that is needed in the UK is touched upon in the description of Popper's open society: that it should be an association or partnership; that it should respect rights and freedom; that the State should be a mutual compact; and that individuals working together should make their own responsible decisions.

8

Trevor Phillips

A View from the Margins

The morning newspapers tell us that Britain is divided; that we no longer share a common purpose as a people, that North confronts South, old are in conflict with young, black alienated from white. And they go on to assert that, because there is no unity, the nation will decline. Around the corner lies collapse.

It's part of our national consciousness to accept that logic. But why? Other nations don't make the equation in the way that we do. The United States, for example comprises 230 million people who divide in myriad ways: geographically, culturally, ethnically, even economically. Yet today's America exhibits probably the strongest freely-established national consensus anywhere in the West. A Reaganite national mood, especially when translated into a landslide win for the Great TV Charmer, isn't to the taste of most Europeans; but it exists, in spite of his relatively hard-line stances on issues of economic principle and social rights. And that consensus, and the confidence that flows from it, is at least in part responsible for the United States' undeniable economic success of the past four years.

The point is that we British resolutely refuse to acknowledge the very real differences within our society. We regard them as a handicap. People may differ only insofar as they do not alter our social norms. Eccentrics are O.K. We can laugh them off; they may even, in an ironic way, reinforce the security of our social norms, whilst reminding us that we are a 'free' society. Iconoclasts, on the other hand, are another matter. It may be that they are geniuses, but if they threaten to change our cosy way of life, then all that goes by the board. Remember the danger associated with almost every youth cult since the war? Cliff Richard and his gyrating hips; Mick Jagger and his pouting lips; Johnny Rotten and his razor-punk rips. They were all portrayed as corrupters and dangers to society as we knew it—before they became as fashionable as Marks and Sparks.

It's my contention that our desire to regard British society as a monolithic bloc united around one ideology or another actually obscures our ability to analyse and to read that society effectively. And as we approach the end of the century, the consequence of that obscurity becomes more dangerous. The reason is that political judgments must be based on an accurate perception of the 'body politic'; without that clear vision our judgments can go disastrously wrong. Witness Alec Douglas-Home's inability in 1963 to perceive the excitement generated by Britain's discovery of 'popular' technology, as expressed through the raising of Sputnik, and through Kennedy's promise to put a man on the moon. The Tories paid for the oversight by surrendering the vital 'modernist' ground to Harold Wilson.

It seems to me that there is a more important reason than our cultural disinclination to accept new ideas that makes us suspicious of differences. It is also an excessive respect for that most fundamental virtue of Tory politics; stability. Most of us associate our personal good with relative stability; and stability prevails where there is political unity. It is only those who feel that there is little left to lose who hanker after radical change. For most Britons, there is clearly a belief that change too often results in something worse than the status quo.

To add to this empirical notion that change usually means personal disadvantage there are political grounds for resisting change. Our system of government is, in practice, based upon an outdated historical notion about what constitutes the British nation. The political culture of both Labour and

Conservative parties is in turn based on the notion that most people identify either with the interests of capital or those of labour. Those who don't identify fully with what the Tories call 'wealth-creation', i.e. the individual accumulation of capital, are seen as anti-patriotic, by both 'wet' and 'dry' Tories; those who fail to pass the Labour test of loyalty to the (undefined) working class are denounced as Tory sympathisers by the new priesthood of the ultra-left.

But in the 1980s, a change of similar magnitude to that recognised by Wilson in the 1960s has taken place, whether we like it or not and whether either side of the political divide recognises it. But it isn't a purely economic, or technologically inspired change. It is much less straight-forward than that, because it has entirely to do with the British nation's perception of itself. What I intend to argue in this chapter is that today, our view of what constitutes the nation is changing, and rightly so. And my contention is that first, we must accept that change is taking place at all; and second, if we perceive that change correctly it will be to our society's advantage. We might be able to frame a new idea of the nation, a new consensus, which is realistically founded upon the diversity and pluralism of the Britain of the future. If we perceive it wrongly it could lead to precisely the kind of social disintegration we fear so greatly.

The prospect in such a situation would not be the classic 'expansion/stability, depression/crisis' cycle. It would be much worse: a life-sapping fragmentation characterised by constant friction between the fragments of our communities.

From where do we start? In my view, by looking at just how the British people's view of themselves has changed, and why.

When all British governments shared what has come to be called the Butskellite consensus, everyone agreed that, in essence, social stability was guaranteed by economic success in which everyone could then share. The post-war expansion of both industrial and service sectors both offered jobs.

It also provided an economic setting that provided for a kind of support system to the poor and deprived that would eliminate the more distressing aspects of society's inequalities from our cities in particular. It seemed, then, that the art of government was efficient management of an expanding economy. Everyone could share in its success either by managing capital or by selling his or her labour.

Politicians of the patrician stamp of Lord Stockton, then Harold Macmillan, inevitably held sway; what was politics, after all, but the exercise of the right sort of authority over this burgeoning economic success, and a proper (though not excessively zealous) distribution of its fruits?

Even the lengthy periods of government by both Conservative and Labour spoke of stability based on prosperity. It is in such periods that those who can't share in that success because they are poor or disadvantaged in some way become a social embarrassment, to be hidden under deluges of social concern and charity. However, the prospect that the social order might genuinely be disrupted in order to remove structural inequalities has always been a non-starter even in the 'good times'. It would, as I suggested before, offer the prospect of change—with the attendant possibility that comfortable people might find themselves not so comfortable.

In fact, the idea of radical political restructuring surfaces most strongly at the times when it becomes in the interests of a large number of people for change to take place— because any change could only be an improvement.

And after nearly thirty years of the old consensus, it was only in the late 1970s that this situation occurred—and Thatcherism became a possibility.

Why?

I believe that three key international issues played a crucial role in changing not only Britain's position in the world, but also Britons' views of their own nation. First, the end of Empire ended Britain's certitude of both economic and cultural hegemony over a large part of the world.

Second, the 1973 oil crisis introduced a further element of doubt about the resilience of Britain's economy in the face of new powers that strode the international stage. And third, the growing global reach and ambitions of the two super powers, particularly the USA under Reagan, have clearly eclipsed us as a nation able to exercise a decisive influence in international affairs.

For a nation whose culture incorporates an extraordinarily high degree of belief in its superiority over the rest of the world, these changes in global relationships are not simply the currency of top politicians. They also affect our everyday lives. The flood of Japanese products into our homes speaks of the rise of 'their' economy and the decline of our own; and the dominating role of American military forces on our own soil reminds us constantly of our subsidiary place in strategic affairs.

A nation whose confidence is already sapped by a change in its place in the world would inevitably find the social and cultural consequences of domestic change even more difficult to cope with. And, perhaps, it is this frame of mind that has left us unprepared and unable to cope with the most dramatic social change in peacetime this century—the prospect of the long-term decline of work.

Reduced competitiveness, a rise in unemployment and most significantly, structural youth unemployment are neither short-term problems, nor are they simply economic phenomena.

The fact that youth unemployment seems to be with us permanently hardly needs to be discussed at length. The statistics show that up to thirty per cent of school leavers in British cities are without work. According to the DES's survey 'Young People in the 80s' (HMSO), forty-five per cent of those not on MSC Schemes had been unemployed for more than six months. These seem uncontestable signs that getting into the labour market is becoming more and more difficult for young people.

The significance of this is profound. Outside the family,

work is undoubtedly the largest single factor in forging individual identity. It offers us purpose; and it offers us a place in the social order. The same survey, 'Young People in the 80s' quoted its finding that for most young people adulthood is only confirmed by employment. Without work, many of the assumptions of the consensus society just cannot apply. Without work, people stop wanting to play the game.

Even amongst those at work, there are divisions. At the top of our social pyramid, the fulfilled, the engaged, the articulate opinion-formers and arbiters of the acceptable are active and engaged. They are true citizens, who all share intense involvement in the processes of our existing society, no matter how much they might disagree with its make-up. To these people—journalists, politicians, businessmen, celebrities of all kinds—work is an end in itself.

Then there are those who have jobs—but to whom work is simply a means to an end—whether it's the summer holiday, the car, or just the mortgage repayments. But in their ordinary life they exercise little influence on the shape or direction of our society. And knowing it, they are content to acquiesce.

But those who have no work to give *them* a place high in the pyramid, and who have no prospect of work, have a very different attitude to society. It is amongst the young unemployed that this difference shows up most sharply.

For most of our young long-term unemployed, the future seems bleak; and they often have a more sophisticated understanding of their problems than their elders.

First, they know that the sunrise industries by which politicians on both sides of the great divide set so much store may well dominate the economic horizon by the turn of the century; but that the employees that those industries will demand will have to possess more skills than the ability to handle a Space Invaders machine. Few of them possess those skills.

Secondly, they see that unemployment is not simply due

to collapsing industries; it's also due to what both unions and managements describe as productivity increases, i.e. higher profits from workers earning more money by producing more units at lower costs by working with more modern machines. And since profits are also used to boost productivity, it seems unlikely that there are going to be more jobs being made available.

And finally, in practice, early retirement and a reduced working week seem to have had very little effect on the prospects for new jobs.

So the young man or woman who is unemployed faces an increasingly marginalised future; there appears to be almost no way into the labour market, and therefore, no way into the existing social order.

Increasingly, this situation is being reflected amongst a growing number of other groups in Britain. And for each group other factors compound their separation from the social consensus. Amongst black people for example, an unpublished national survey for London Weekend Television showed an unemployment rate, amongst those eligible for work, of thirty per cent overall, rising to forty per cent for those under 24. In Northern Ireland, the situation amongst both Catholic and Protestant communities is equally bad. And in all three cases, the alienation of the communities is profound; and it is expressed in direct hostility to the agencies most identifiable as the protectors of state interests—the police and the Army.

We could add to those who are moving outside of the consensual orbit for different reasons many ordinary people who may not themselves be unemployed, but who belong to communities whose culture is infected by the bitterness and hostility of long-term unemployment.

What I mean by the term 'infected' can easily be explained with reference to the black community's hostility to the police, a clear sign of alienation from the State and all its workings. According to one survey, only one in three young black people claim that they have had any direct experience with the police; yet nine out of ten say that they 'mistrust and fear' the police. It's clear that the hostility of those who may, for example, have been stopped and searched whilst standing in the street (a common experience for those out of work) has been passed on to their friends and peers. In this way, it has come to be established as a group phenomenon.

There's little doubt that similar processes are at work in Northern Ireland, and in certain areas of the North of England, where certain communities are seeing themselves more and more as having been cut off from the centre of the social consensus represented by London.

So what is the consequence of the creeping marginalisation of large sections of the nation, first by unemployment and secondly by what I have described as the infection of a group's culture?

To many in the political arena, this process represents an opportunity. The GLC, for example, has capitalised heavily on social fragmentation. Ken Livingstone, an acutely sensitive observer of the political scene, leapt into action with support for pressure groups which symbolise the disaffection of ethnic groups and the unemployed.

But, of course, the hope of the Labour left is to exploit that disaffection by binding marginalised groupings into an alliance with orthodox labour organisations. The enterprise, politically attractive as it may seem, is doomed for two reasons. The first lies in the conservatism of labour, which, frankly speaking, would like to have as little as possible to do with ethnic and radical pressure groups as possible. The second lies in the nature of the marginalisation process itself.

The fact is, none of these people voluntarily cut themselves off from the consensus. In most cases, what they would like most of all is to belong. It is the pressure of factors beyond their control that pushes them out. Black people, for example, would be happy to take their place in society, if only the racism that permeates our institutions would allow them to be employed, judged, and otherwise dealt with on the same basis as everyone else. Added to which is a deep cynicism amongst the young and the black about the trade union movement; their suspicion is born of long experience that the British trade union movement will fight for you—as long as you are a member. Of course, that is what unions are for. But if your interests as an unemployed worker or a non-unionist don't coincide with those of the unionists, you can expect little help. This is hardly the material from which comes the movement that transforms the society in the way that Labour's left would like. It is not a yearning for a reshaping of society. It is rather the outpouring of a desire to share in the fruits of what exists. This is the truth that all radicals and reformers must face. There is no insurrectionary road to change based on alienated groupings.

On the other hand, there is no comfort to be drawn from the thought that the steadily growing numbers of people in these marginalised groupings will simply sit still and wait for things to become better. Far from it. Instead, what we have created is a steadily growing underclass, always destined to be composed of a fragmented set of minority groups, but always certain to be an irritant. They are an irritant because in a fair and equal society they should not be marginalised; and they are an irritant because they are a reminder of our failure to create that fair and equal society.

In the 1930s war solved the problem. Today, war would achieve quite the opposite. But unless we do solve it, major problems arise for Government. The nature of those problems is rooted in the divisions that this essay discusses.

In terms of engagement and attachment for our existing democracy we could end up with a society enfeebled both economically and politically; divided between the included and complacent, and the excluded and angry; and with a steadily crumbling attachment to a democratic consensus. It is this that I see as the greatest danger of marginalisation.

So what other answers are there?

I have already dealt with one political alternative: the Labour left attempt to co-opt marginalised groups. This will be unsuccessful. The alternative, Thatcherite, strategy is equally cynical. It gambles on marginalisation never being significant enough to challenge the grip of its 'natural' majority. Thus unemployed people can be stigmatised as weak, uncompetitive or scrounging; black people as alien or criminal; and the Irish as simply irrational. The 'united nation' which Mrs Thatcher seeks to lead would simply exclude these marginal deviants. But that won't do either. The larger the marginalised groups grow, the less credible the smears become. So another answer has to be found.

This is not the place in which to advance extensive economic prescriptions. However, we can take some lead from the very people we have marginalised. In one small area of our national life, at least, there may be a glimmer of a way out.

It is clear that no matter how much many young people may wish to find their way into work, it is not going to be there for all of them. And the longer the period during which they try and fail to enter the orthodox labour market the more apathetic and alienated they become. Though this won't lead to insurrection it could have another tragic result. But amongst the unemployed there are young people of immense talent and enterprise in economic areas that are expanding in world terms, and in which Britain has always been internationally competitive. I have in mind the creative areas of the economy—popular music and art, publishing, fashion, computer software, entertainment, film-making, design, even sport. There are also people who might add some bite in areas where Britain desperately needs top-class talent—sales and marketing. Yet the opportunities for exploitation of that raw talent is small. Most of the entertainment and leisure industry is in the hands of gigantic monopolies who dictate taste and style and indeed shape the market to their own needs.

Small, independent talents, unless they find a very particular and as yet unexploited niche, stand little chance of success against these giants. The result is that unless you happen to catch the eye of the big company executive, your chances of developing your talents are small.

We should be encouraging and fostering enterprise of this kind, by doing two things. First, we should restrict the power of the monopoly to control markets where individual enterprise could otherwise flower. Second, we should offer more support to training and enterprise in those areas of the economy. It is, for example, an absurdity that the UK popular record market is dominated by American subsidiaries when (even in the age of Michael Jackson) British artists hold a disproportionately large share of sales internationally.

The reality is that as a nation we fear to recognise that those we have left out of the scheme of things may have a genuine contribution to make. They are different from us only by force of circumstance. It's time we began to nurture the talents of the 'different' amongst us.

In the long run it could be the only way to avoid social disintegration. But that would take a new attitude to the prospect of change; and it would mean the inclusion of the excluded in our neat scheme of things. Have we the courage to welcome and encourage diversity within our new consensus?

9

John Alderson

Police and the Social Order

Few benefits are more important to a civilised society than a degree of public tranquillity which allows the individual full enjoyment of his freedom and security. In achieving such a desirable condition the role of the police system and its place in the social order is obviously central. However it should be emphasised that a police system is but the product and a reflection of a society's values at a particular time and in a particular place, rather than the other way round. In this sense a society really does get the police it deserves. There are both historic and contemporary examples to support this axiom.

Nor should we forget that a society may seek to diminish as well as to extend the role of its official police. It is not inevitable that public tranquillity should require a constant extension of police power and a concomitant diminution of liberty and erosion of personal civic obligation, participation and duty.

To define the proper place of policing in society, a small historical digression may be helpful. We owe the origin of the term 'police' to the Greeks, stemming as it does from their *polis*, the city, and *politeia*, a comprehensive term describing the safety and the welfare of the inhabitants. The *politeia* in the Greek city-state was within the concern and influence of all citizens as a collective and democratic responsibility. The Romans, having adopted and latinised the term into *politia*, placed the power which it represented with the Emperor under the fiction of imperial sovereignty.

Police power was regarded by the Romans as lying at the heart of state authority.

It is interesting how some of the contemporary debate on policing around the world mirrors the competing ideas of Greek and Roman in this regard. The existing French police system leans to Rome, whilst the British leans, albeit perhaps less than it should, towards ancient Athens. The British system is the product of several historical factors: early tribal custom; a strong tradition of local government and later of democratic local government; and nine hundred years of evolution free from conquest and alien rule. Sadly, traditional British values of policing have become an endangered species. The Romans are gaining ground.

To say that the British system leans a little towards the ancient city-state of Athens is a way to emphasise that in Britain police power has never been regarded as lying at the heart of state authority. Moreover the wider meaning of police, in the Greek sense of the general safety and welfare of the inhabitants, embraces the concept of the maintenance of a tolerable social order within the influence of many and varied democratic institutions. Room has to be left in the vocabulary of the policing debate for both meanings. More of one, the wider, may mean less of another, the narrower.

In believing that in some ways our policing is at a watershed, I do so out of the conviction that the social order is itself at a watershed. This follows from my earlier assertion that a policing system reflects the values which a society places upon itself.

The term 'police state' has always aroused strong emotions for British people. Today it has once again entered the political vocabulary. But what sort of police state are we talking about? At one extreme lies the totalitarian model. Yet might not the route to repression in Britain more probably be that of Lord Hailsham's 'elective dictatorship', seized by radical authoritarianism?

If Britain is moving towards a kind of police state it is more likely to arrive at a destination which is generally feared and disliked through drift and democratic decline than through a positive ideological commitment to state power backed by force. This of course makes it more difficult to identify and therefore to combat. Contemporary Britain manifests a number of disturbing symptoms which could contribute to this drift towards a 'police state'. They include:

Stunted democracy
Bureaucratic centralism
Absence of a Bill of Rights
Weakening of local government
Increase in agents of central government e.g. inspectors and investigators
Police accountability not satisfactorily defined
Central control of the system of criminal prosecutions
Widening of the definition of 'subversion'
The labelling of activists and protesters as 'anti-social bodies'
Acquisition and storage of non-criminal intelligence shared between government departments including the security services and the police
Authoritarian government impregnable in Parliament
Apathy in society regarding these things
A weak political centre.

Ten years ago the distinguished historian, the late Arnold Toynbee, writing in the *Observer* said, 'The economic deterioration in developed countries indicates the onset of a new way of life, a severely regimented way of life which would have to be imposed by a ruthless authoritarian government.' Our economic deterioration is generally admitted, although its extent and future direction is the subject of political debate. No consideration of the police and the social order can evade the connection with the economic state of the nation.

Although eighty per cent of the work force may be

enjoying comparative affluence at the present, sufficient for the large majority to be reasonably content, some twenty per cent, or one in five, are not. The declining asset of North Sea oil has so far cushioned the effect. I do not hear the ranks of the economists forecasting a certain continuance of Western prosperity. I have seen the growing prosperity of East Asia for myself. The balance of world economic ascendancy may be shifting. The effect for Britain, already one of the weakest Western economies, will be particularly severe and the strains are already showing.

The capacity of the economy to sustain both increases in untaxed income and maintenance of the health and social security benefits and services must be in doubt. The rising cost of state pensions, index-linked and extrapolated, causes Treasury officials to wince. One does not need to be an economist to consider the social consequences of economic deterioration.

I agree with Toynbee that a nation beset by the trauma of dramatic economic deterioration and change faces the possibility, though not necessarily the certainty, of both disorder and ruthless authoritarian government. Economics and policing are related in more ways than one. It is no longer fanciful to pose the question whether continuing economic deterioration will destroy the prospect for policing by consent. After all, the urban poor of London in 1829 were not policed by consent, and to suggest otherwise would be to court ridicule.

Is our social order adaptable enough to avoid Toynbee's prediction? His ruthless authoritarian government would require a strong arm capable of executing its purpose, namely the police, and of course in the last resort the army. Such a role for the police in Britain is against our recent traditions. Nevertheless we have been acquiring over the last twenty-five years a police organisation which could quite easily be converted into an offensive arm for such a government. It is a highly mobile force with excellent national communications, data banks and an intelligence system. It is well armed, possessing the appropriate riot equipment including the dreaded plastic bullet. It has developed highly trained companies of riot police with the best protective equipment.

All these enhancements of power can be justified individually, but taken together they raise the question of control in the most critical way. In the technological sense control is as advanced as any of the national forces on the Continent and elsewhere. Nor is there any shortage of legal powers, which are soon to be strengthened, even though administrative checks on abuse are proposed. Emergency regulations could be readily passed by Parliament to give further essential powers.

On the police side there would be little likelihood of widespread disaffection. It is a well disciplined organisation, comparatively highly paid and tight knit. The police would be able to serve the authoritarian regime. However the police ideologically lean more to the authoritarian right than to the authoritarian left. This is partly due to innate conservatism and partly to the fact that the ideologists of the far left have a long tradition of criticising the police as part of an established order which they despise and wish to change. By the same token the far right tends not to criticise the police, even for admitted shortcomings or excesses, believing that, regrettable though they may be, criticism would tend to weaken the police as part of an establishment which they wish to see strengthened.

If Toynbee's ruthless authoritarian government came from the right there would be few problems in converting the existing police system to its purposes. This is a fact which may give comfort to some and discomfort to others. If, on the other hand, such a government came from the left there could be problems which would arise not from the technical and legal arrangements but from the ideological and political preferences of some police officials. Some chief officers and police spokesmen in England (I am not aware of any in Scotland) have made no secret of their dislike of the politics and policies of the left and by extension of local control. The Police Federation in England and Wales and the Police Superintendents' Association have retained Conservative Members of Parliament as their advisers, and for many years now have abandoned the convention of retaining a member of Her Majesty's Opposition. Their political campaigns between and during general elections have coincided closely with those of the Conservative manifesto.

Increased penal severity, capital punishment, tighter measures for dealing with juvenile offenders, increases in police power, and severance of the police from local government have all been the subject of campaigns or public speeches by police spokesmen. It is, on the other hand, fair to say that the police have in general steered clear of party political intrigue. In this sense we are fortunate.

It may of course be that Toynbee's scenario will not come to pass, even if economic deterioration causes social convulsions. We may be blessed, before it is too late, with leaders who develop a political system and philosophy to match the times. When all is said and done the British are amongst the most governable of people. We must not test that governability to its limits.

Contemporary society is not in good shape to take severe economic strain without considerable prospects for crime and disorder. Those parts and characteristics of the social order which stood for homogeneity and consensus have gradually been weakened as the impulses which fuel social dynamism have found their outlets in social mobility. The new demography finds its principal common expression in widespread materialism.

People will not give up hard won privileges easily. Nor will the assertive accept with docility what they perceive to be injustice or unfairness. Envy, that running mate of greed, is rife. When a society develops in this way, as many Western societies have in recent times, people begin to rely more on the law to provide discipline and stability rather than depending on traditions of social cohesion and fraternity. 'Land of Hope and Glory' is still sung, though more in a spirit of nostalgia than reality, and never in certain of our deprived areas and the schools located within them.

Whilst the political parties struggle for ascendancy the nation divides in deepening bitterness. Perhaps it cannot yet be said that iron has entered the soul of Britain, but there is now iron in enough souls to warrant plausible arguments for preparing the police to cope with tougher times.

In order to comprehend and cope with some of the uglier aspects of an unhappy society Mrs Thatcher and her likeminded supporters have counselled not a going-forward to develop new social values but a return to the old deference. But there can be no going back. Of course it would make control of people easier if each person kept his station and did as he or she was told, accepted seeming injustices, unfair division of goods and labour, and obeyed the police without question. But Britain's coalfields and depressed areas of former industrial cities manifested more assertive than submissive tendencies in 1984, providing examples of what could become a familiar pattern. The conflict may involve the police, the courts and the penal system to an extent we have not previously witnessed in Britain.

In a passive, submissive society, particularly where consensus prevails, policing is a comparatively straightforward task, but when whole parts of a society begin to mount a challenge to authoritarianism, policing becomes more burdensome, particularly at the point where the challenge mounts and authoritarianism shows no sign of flexibility or responsiveness.

This represents a turning point, since if those possessed of political power decline to use it to meet widespread demand for changes, the police will be called upon to play a major role in maintaining the status quo. It is likely that in such a condition two societies will emerge, the privileged and the deprived, and that prospects for the eruption of communal violence will consequently increase. The police operate at this interface since they are on the side of the status quo and will both suffer violence from, and apply it to, the dissenters.

The 1981 riots in London and other English cities may have been fuelled by adverse social conditions but they were ignited by police practice. This is the essential lesson to be learnt from the Scarman Inquiry. People will put up with a lot in the way of social deprivation without resorting to violence, for they often have a propensity to blame themselves for their predicament. However, when their predicament is compounded by what seems to be unduly repressive policing the breaking point will be reached much earlier than it otherwise would.

It may well be that the absence of anti-police riots in Scottish cities in 1981, despite equally severe unemployment, reflects less repressive police policies, a more community orientated social order, fewer cultural differences, or greater homogeneity. If this be the case it goes some way towards proving much of my thesis. Sensitive use of police becomes even more important where social conditions are bad. Where social conditions are good, insensitive use of police will result in complaints through formal channels provided for such contingencies. Where they are bad they will result in riot.

It gives me no satisfaction to say that two years before the riots in England I wrote, drawing attention to this social phenomenon, in the following terms: 'The decaying inner-city areas are breeding grounds for crime and disaffection. To leave them to the vagaries of law enforcement would be unwise. There are now sufficient examples of how neglected social problems which have been allowed to fester to a dangerous state, but which have been covered over and policed by force, can break out in public disorder. In such cases the police are trapped in a dilemma. On the one hand they perceive (or should perceive, I may add) the problems but, not having a solution, they gradually become a solution of expediency, though sooner or later social repair and reconstruction has to begin. From a police point of view the sooner the better.' Policing can otherwise too easily become part of the problem. The police system is no longer as capable as it was of responding to social diversity, of grasping the character of small communities in their varied circumstances, needs and desires. Where there is no dialogue there can be no understanding, where there is no accountability there is no compulsion to serve. Both these assertions apply *pari passu* to many other government services. To examine the issues critically is not to blame the police.

The more complex a social order becomes, the more the services which tend to its needs require the flexibility to adapt to local as well as regional and national circumstances. Unfortunately there is a fatal divergence of interest and perception on this matter. Thus whilst British society has become infinitely more diversified and pluralistic, the services upon which it depends, including the police, have become more remote and bureaucratic.

Policies which are developed by large bureaucracies remote from local diversity and sentiment do not always fit the kaleidoscopic variety of needs of the ultimate beneficiaries. An example of this divergence is to be found in the evidence of the Commissioner of Police of the Metropolis to Lord Scarman's Inquiry on the Brixton riots in London. The policies of the Force, it was claimed, had been reviewed in the wake of the riots and it was felt that there was no need to change them. The Inquiry, and subsequent police reflection, however, found that in the particular locality the policing policies had been a major factor in producing communal reaction on a serious scale.

Any examination of the divergence between community needs and bureaucratic distance, so far as the policing system is concerned, has to begin with changes in the structure of local government. After all, our policing is based upon local government.

The creation of larger units of local government in Great

Britain following upon the Local Government Acts of 1972 (in England and Wales) and 1973 (in Scotland) greatly enlarged police bureaucracies. The police of Strathclyde and Greater Manchester could no longer, by any stretch of the imagination, be called local police forces. In going for the benefits of scale, and there are some which are real including better use of resources and coordination of effort, local roots and accountability were needlessly sacrificed. Although District Councils, and in Scotland (though not in England and Wales) Community Councils, provided a role for the immediate locality in some aspects of government, they were to have no role as far as policing was concerned. Great and ancient cities and towns were to be policed by regionally administered forces. At the same time the de-localisation of the police was compounded by the trend towards greater professionalism in the force.

By police professionalism I mean the dangerous concept that the role of the police in the social order should be defined by the police. When the weakening of local influence is combined with professional certitude, the way is opened up for the police to become an institution in itself.

The police system is felt to have become so large and complex that only the police can understand and define its purpose. The development of police technology gives a further seductive tug in the same direction. Sophisticated computer-directed responses, new and impressive mobility and technological systems of modern communication can all help to create a feeling within the organisation that it possesses the power to be efficient without relying on seemingly old-fashioned notions of *politeia* or public participation and influence. These illusions of omnipotence are more marked in some systems abroad than in Britain, but there are ominous signs of a drift in this direction here, too.

Recent research has, for example, confirmed that, so far as the detection of crime is concerned, no less than eighty-five per cent of reported cases are detected wholly or in part by the public. The police compile the reports and collect the evidence. This suggests that in clearing up crime police technology is less important than public contact and support.

Research carried out jointly in Devon and Cornwall and Greater Manchester highlighted a very significant discrepancy in perception of the role of the police between the public and the force itself. Whereas the public tended to judge delivery of police services in terms of the human qualities, skills, understanding and problem solving, the police officers believed they were being judged on their technological modernity and reactive efficiency in, for example, responding quickly and activating the police machine. The result was that the police over-estimated the public regard for the way in which they functioned. This is an ominous trend if not in some way corrected.

The problems of scale, remoteness of local government administration of the police, and the growth of police professionalism have all contributed to misunderstanding, conflict and uncertainty about the place of the police in the social order. This is not good for the police nor as reassuring for the public as it might be. Police authorities have found difficulty in knowing how to meet the requirement for accountability which the system provides for. The dilemma, and one police authority's response, was expressed by Margaret Simey, chairperson of the Merseyside Authority, in the following terms: 'The message which emerged from the mini-Scarman Inquiry conducted by the Merseyside Police Authority after the disturbances of 1981 was that it was democracy which had failed the people of Toxteth and not the police. Put bluntly it was the failure of the police authority to fulfil its political duty to ensure that the people were policed by their own wishes, so far as was possible, which had brought the situation to flashpoint.'

Margaret Simey's comment that 'it was democracy that failed the people' is an arresting one, an informed and sagacious insight. It draws our attention to the inexorable truth that weakness in democratic activity opens the door to injustice and the misuse of power. In its extreme form, it can expose liberty and justice to a total and crushing defeat. But there are degrees of damage, short of democratic defeat, which are already being inflicted on our society.

The state of democracy in Britain today is germane to the subject before us. Democracy in Britain is too stunted to warrant optimism or to justify complacency. From apex to base there are weaknesses.

The House of Lords makes no pretension to being a democratic institution whatever its other virtues may be, and it has many. Yet at the same time the assembly of the House of Commons, our bulwark, currently fails to reflect the growing diversity of political opinion among the electorate. Anxiety in this regard is reflected in broad agreement among some members of all political parties that there should be some reform of the voting system. The winner-takes-all system may strengthen the government of the day but it alienates the loyalties of the voters at large. It serves power at the expense of democracy.

The picture is no rosier at local government level. Not only is it not 'local' any more but it is being weakened and demoralised by the radicalism of central government. This is a conflict which is likely to intensify. There is a huge vacuum at community and neighbourhood level and it is here that the lack of means for democratic participation encourages the proponents of direct action.

The trade unions are also at bay—partly due to the abuse of their power which has weakened their moral authority and the respect in which they are held, and partly due to the same radicalism of the present government which has been devastatingly combined with the threat of unemployment. When democracy is weak or abused, greater recourse to repression by those charged with government becomes all too probable.

Another weakness in our democratic system which becomes more obvious as bureaucratic power increases is the absence of a Bill of Rights to protect individuals and groups. Although Britain was a founder member of the Council of Europe and one of the architects of the Convention on Human Rights, we have singularly failed to train our police and other officials in its spirit and purpose.

This combination of defective democracy, absence of a Bill of Rights enshrined in our domestic laws, economic deterioration and laissez-faire leading to a divided nation, is likely to increase reliance on the use of criminal sanctions. This in turn will mean increases in repression and surveillance, thus fundamentally shifting the place of the police in the social order.

I have briefly opened up constitutional questions, which are comprehensively dealt with by Richard Holme in Chapter 7, because of the special relevance of a healthy democracy to policing by consent. But for the last part of my contribution I intend to concentrate on the problem of anchoring the police to the communities which they serve. I believe that if they are so anchored they themselves will gain much. They will feel more secure as an institution, they will receive more public help and guidance in the delivery of their services. A way will be opened for local democratic impulses in society to balance the growth of anonymous bureaucratic power.

For all kinds of reasons, apart from policing, the creation of Community Forums is a pressing need. In a confident expanding society people may feel able to disengage from mutuality. In a contracting and apprehensive society mutuality assumes greater importance. If this movement towards mutual help could succeed, it would offer a counter to the other expedient of excessive reliance on the strong leader. The former, communitarianism that is, strengthens the social order whilst preserving freedom and developing democratic participation, whereas the latter, the strong leader, requires the sacrifice of independent local judgement.

Community Forum areas would be drawn up on a definitive map by local authorities. Residents would appoint delegates, not representatives, street by street. Delegates would be preferable to representatives to avoid undue politicisation. To make them manageable, at least in the cities and towns, Community Forums would serve between ten and twenty thousand inhabitants.

Participation in community affairs would be an individual right. A programme of education, both for the young and the adult, would be designed to stimulate understanding and participation.

Into these primary cells of democracy, the police and other agencies providing a community service would be locked. The welfare and safety of the inhabitants would provide the terms of reference.

In due course such forums would number tens of thousands, some more active and well conducted than others no doubt. The well-springs of democratic activity would in this way be primed. This would not be another tier of government but a forum or platform to generate local initiative, action and concern. A Minister for Community Affairs and local government Community Affairs Committees would share the responsibility for setting up and nurturing them.

As for the police, the secondary level of their accountability would be at district level, where consultative groups set up for the purpose would provide this link. Following upon Lord Scarman's recommendations, a statutory duty to create these groups in England and Wales is included in the Police and Criminal Evidence Bill at present before Parliament. The third level of police accountability would rest, as it does, formally with the police authorities at what I call regional level.

It should be emphasised that the police role in the social order is primarily that of keepers of the peace, and preventers of crime. This function can only be exercised successfully in neighbourhoods and local communities. It is here that police officers have to toil in the foothills of the social order. The enforcement of law is additional to this primary function and must not usurp it. The success of our *politeia* should not be judged by the efficiency with which we can build larger prisons, increase penal severity, and enlarge the population of detention centres and prisons. It should rather be judged by our success in relying less on criminal sanctions to protect the social order and more on innovation and ideas of preventive activity in those primary cells of the body politic represented by the local communities of Britain. But none of this is likely to come about in isolation. Co-operation in civic fraternity depends on a partnership society which generates fraternal impulses. The division of goods and labour has to be seen to be fair, democracy in all its forms must be improved, human rights should be enshrined in the constitution, bureaucratic centralism must be tamed and controlled, and the powers which could otherwise create a 'kind of police state' must be adequately accountable.

All the signs are that in the foreseeable future Britain's police traditions will be seriously tested. They would be better served by an increase in democracy and a decrease in the prospects of violent conflict. The plea for a change in direction by the Year 2000 might have bemused an Imperial Roman but it would have been well understood by an Ancient Athenian.

10

David Steel

Britain's Place in the World

The most distressing aspect of Britain's post-war history has been our failure to define our place in the world. Dean Acheson summed it up admirably when he said, 'Britain has lost an empire and has not yet found a role.'

A nation in the sunset of empire, drained by two world wars and two decades of economic strife between them, was in no position to remain blindly aloof in the much altered circumstances of post-1945. Yet that is what we did. Europe looked to Britain for a lead to rebuild a united Continent. We failed to respond. Many of our problems since then stem from that first failure.

Despite protests from the small band of Liberals in Parliament, successive governments stumbled along, with no clear sense of direction or purpose. Churchill wanted Britain to remain an island 'with Europe, but not of them', over-estimating Britain's capacity for survival in isolation and under-estimating the strengths of our neighbours; Attlee and Macmillan both played on a 'special relationship' with the Americans from which we lost out heavily; Douglas-Home and Wilson were at best agnostic about Britain's place in the world, prepared to maintain the illusions that we were an independent world power, despite the lesson of Suez; it was left to Ted Heath finally to grasp the nettle and take us into Europe, better late than never, and both Labour and Tory governments since then have behaved as if they resented our membership—threatening withdrawal, haggling over budgets, being ever the reluctant and sulking partner in what for others was an exciting new venture.

The failure of our political leaders to understand world developments since 1945 correctly has led Britain to adopt the wrong policies towards both our European neighbours and the USA. We have similarly failed to find the right defence and disarmament policy or to define proper relations with the developing countries as we retreat from Empire. These misjudgements have had a damaging effect on our economy, our welfare and education systems and the values and structures we use for policy making, as I will illustrate later.

Britain's arrogant and blinkered attitude in world affairs was aptly illustrated by the decision to send only an observer from the Board of Trade to the conference at Messina where the idea of European Union was first discussed. As the Liberal Leader, Clement Davies, said in Parliament at the time:

> 'Are we standing on one side and not co-operating with those countries, who have so much at stake? It would ease their position very much if we helped one another economically and had better communications. What is of even greater importance is that what I call the "Schuman Plan" works. Unfortunately, we have stood outside.'

From the outset Liberals have been committed to a united Europe. For many years we were an isolated voice, shunned by those who preferred to turn their backs on a Europe whose institutions and policies were being fashioned without British influence.

Alone of the British political parties we were not frightened to acknowledge that there might be limits to parliamentary sovereignty. We did not fear supranational co-operation. Time and time again we have stressed the political value of European integration, because we have seen it as a step towards wider international co-operation and a more secure world.

That said, there is much that is wrong with the European Community. Its present framework of institutions and policies requires radical reform. What was right for a community of six centred on the European mainland is hardly appropriate for the present membership of ten: a community of twelve, to which we are now committed, will need to be a much more flexible federation, concentrating on the guidelines of policy at the centre and leaving the details of implementation to the States themselves. If this is possible in a developed federation like the United States, it should not be impossible for a looser confederation like the European Community.

We cannot pretend that there will be a return to much more rapid economic growth within the foreseeable future to enable European countries to avoid facing up to some of the awkward choices which the current recession has forced on us. We cannot return to the years of cheap raw materials and cheap energy; indeed, despite the current oil glut, all the signs are that both raw materials and energy will become progressively dearer and scarcer. The European economy must adjust to a world in which competition for markets is fiercer, the threat of protectionism sharper, and the needs of the developing countries more pressing if they are not oil-producers. That requires more positive economic policies, and greater political authority for the Community's institutions.

The crisis of the Community's institutions does not—as Chancellor Schmidt used to suggest—primarily reflect the inefficiencies and extravagances of the European Commission. It is far more the responsibility of national governments, increasingly preoccupied with domestic advantage, decreasingly willing to give a lead to their own domestic opinion. It is not only in Britain that public support for European co-operation has declined in the last few years, to a point where it represents a serious obstacle to any positive new initiative; the reassertion of nationalism is evident in France, and can be seen not far below the surface within the German electorate. Political leaders have been reluctant to explain to their electorates the need for European co-operation, for sacrificing immediate national interests for the greater advantages to be gained through common action, and through contributing from hard-pressed national budgets to the common funds. Political imagination and political leadership, of an order not seen within the Community since the oil crisis of 1973, will be needed if we are to move forward.

There are three broad policy areas in which closer European co-operation is now urgently needed: in economic and industrial policy, in external relations and on environmental issues with which I dealt in Chapter 5. The Liberal Party has urged the United Kingdom to join fully in the European Monetary System since its inception, and has reasserted its commitment within the context of a deliberate attempt to find a stable international exchange rate for sterling. But we do not find monetarism any more attractive at the European level than at the national. Monetary co-operation can only be one part of a wider package of economic and industrial policies; a refusal by governments to admit this can only result in leaving EMS stuck at its initial stage. Economic union implies a framework for industrial policies at the Community level, not only for such crisis sectors as textiles and steel, but also for the new technologies into which European industry must be encouraged to move. It implies substantial transfers of resources from the richer to the poorer regions, to compensate for the advantages which the Community's most successful regions draw from the creation of an integrated market. It implies closer co-ordination of domestic economic policies, so that sharply differing rates of inflation, growth and employment do not undermine the achievements of the monetary co-operation and of the integrated market itself. It requires closer scrutiny of the hidden protectionist practices of member governments, and an extension of the open-market principle to the financial and service sectors in which such self-proclaimed 'free-traders' as Federal Germany remain so stubbornly protective. All of this, in turn, will require a substantial strengthening of the Community's political authority and legitimacy.

In an international recession and darkening international political scene, closer co-operation in external economic relations and in foreign policy is now needed. It will be difficult to manage economic relations with the United States and Japan, vigorously competing for command of the new technologies and dominance of the international market, without a strengthened capacity for external negotiation backed by more integrated policies within the Community.

With American leadership less benevolent and with the Soviet Union retreating from détente to Russian imperialism, European political co-operation is likely to prove inadequate in its present form. I welcomed the proposals of my Liberal colleague, Hans-Dietrich Genscher, for a new treaty on European political union, to provide the mechanisms and the authority for more integrated action in the foreign policy sphere. This question now heads the agenda.

A Community, with the authority to act in the central political fields of economic and industrial co-operation and of foreign policy, will also need greater legitimacy and more efficient political institutions. Liberals have welcomed the first efforts of the democratically elected European Parliament to assert its authority over the Community budget and the balance of the Community policies, while protesting at the absence of democratic electoral procedures which has so far excluded us from participating in their debates.

A decision on a common electoral system for the European Parliament has twice been sabotaged by the Conservatives who have played on the difficulties of finding a system of proportional representation on which various countries and party groups can agree. It is imperative that the Parliament should rapidly reach a compromise and put its system to the Council of Ministers. Another election in 1988 on a discredited first-past-the-post system would be a disaster. By contrast a fairly elected Parliament, representative of the different peoples and parties of Europe, would have a new authority and momentum in the decades ahead.

Sadly, national governments have failed to agree on even modest proposals for strengthening and reforming the European Commission. It makes sense to build on the institutions which we have, rather than attempting to start afresh; but that requires substantial reform, not only of the Commission but also of the operating procedures of the Council of Ministers and of the European Council (summit) system. It also implies that the major political institutions of the Community must be brought physically together in one city, so that Parliament can exercise effective scrutiny over the Community executive.

Europe does not need any new constitutional blueprint. What it needs is a renewed commitment to co-operation in the central policies which concern national governments, rather than excessive preoccupation with agriculture and the harmonisation of trading regulations.

The reappearance of external threats, both to Europe's security and to its economic prosperity, carries the danger that the Community will collapse into economic nationalism and political fragmentation; but it also carries the incentive for a closer collaboration and an upgrading of the common interest. Which choice it takes depends upon the qualities of imagination and leadership displayed by politicians inside and outside the governments of the member states. We must provide a lead to domestic opinion to rediscover the advantages of European co-operation, and to press others in Britain and elsewhere to take the imaginative leap towards a redefined European union capable of managing the economic and political pressures that will confront us in the next fifteen years. A two-speed Europe, with

Britain on the slow track, would be damaging to Europe as well as to Britain.

It is our future in Europe which must determine our relations with the United States. The Churchillian myth that Britain can stand up on her own to the United States (and to Europe) is long since dead. Only by playing a wholehearted role in the EEC can we withstand the winds of change and compete successfully with our cousins across the Atlantic. Looking back, I doubt that the lend–lease aid programme was beneficial in the long run. And Truman's 'Grand Area Plan', which foresaw the US takeover of the Middle Eastern oil interests and other Third-World resources of the declining European powers, was hardly designed to help Europe. (Britain in fact viewed US aid at the time with considerable suspicion: in a parliamentary debate on 13th December 1945, 100 M.P.s opposed the terms of the American loan and 169 abstained.)

Neither should we expect any American altruism today in our trading or currency relations. Where the US multinationals moved into Britain in the 1960s, with all the inevitable outcry, British firms did the same in America in the 1970s. The much vaunted 'special relationship' between Britain and America, which flourished in the hearts of our peoples, has been handled less shrewdly by British governments than by American. It is striking that Mrs Thatcher on her visits to the United States has tended to be an echo for the views of the White House and has failed to put forward British and European interests with full vigour.

Western economies are now more interdependent than ever before and we trade—within rules mutually agreed in the GATT framework—as competitors, even if for security reasons we are members of the same military Alliance.

Co-operation in defence and security matters provides the major bond between Europe and America. While there has been much discontent over the years (on both sides of the Atlantic) with NATO, its surprising success has been its ability to survive the sometimes choppy seas. Stormier waters lie ahead, however.

Many Americans are asking aloud whether risking the survival of their nation, at a huge cost, is worth the continuing defence of an ungrateful Europe. And, in their turn, many Europeans wonder whether their security lies in being tied to an American administration which too often seems aggressive, insensitive to human rights abuses, and lacking in self-control.

I do not share the view of Neil Kinnock that there is an 'equity of menace' between the Superpowers. Nor can Liberals ever be neutral in the struggle between the liberal values of a free society and the forces of totalitarianism. But I do believe that there is scope for turning European fears into a more positive recognition both of a common security role and for the need to be, in the words of former Italian Prime Minister Spadolini, 'a protagonist for détente'.

At the heart of the issue is the question of European defence co-operation.

We must not overlook the distance between the aspirations of the European defence dialogue and the strategic realities. The firing of Cruise and Pershing missiles depends entirely on the US President—we still do not have the dual key that the Americans have been proposing for twenty-five years now (for the Thor and Jupiter missiles). The US remains the only Western power with second-strike nuclear capability on land, sea and in the air. And the US defines the doctrine and the consequences of NATO strategy.

To face the challenges of the 1980s, however, the need to transform NATO into a partnership of equals, where a European pillar provides a counterbalance to the American force, becomes ever more urgent. The Liberal call to the government to support the plan for a European Defence Community in 1952 was rejected.

Britain must not make the same mistake again; the current Franco-German defence dialogue and the revival of the Western European Union offers a new opportunity to work together with our European neighbours. It is one which we must grasp. The expansion of the EEC, with the accession of Portugal and Spain, may provide the opportunity.

An enlarged Community will mean that eleven out of NATO's sixteen states will be political partners in the EEC as well as military allies in NATO. That Community will have a population of over 300 million, will be technologically advanced, relatively prosperous and with developing common institutions. Europe already makes a major contribution to its own defence—providing over ninety per cent of the ground forces, eighty per cent of the main battle tanks and two thirds of the major ships in the European sphere of operations. It is time that the logic of a single European voice on defence matters was properly developed.

It was partly the failure of our government to cultivate such a unified voice which led to the need to send a massive Task Force to the Falklands in 1982.

The war in the South Atlantic has had an enduring impact on British defence policy. At its most obvious, it provided a vivid testament to the bravery, skill and professionalism of the armed forces. After the politicians had failed, it was left to the military to provide a military success.

But wider lessons are being learnt as well. For example, some have argued that the campaign proved the ability of the United Kingdom to pursue an independent role in the world. On the contrary, I believe that the war underlined the need for important areas of co-operation with our allies, not least in communications and technological matters. The illusion of independent action could not even have been sustained a year later—and there was no doubt that the support of the United States was crucial in securing victory.

But it is the long-term legacy of the Falklands conflict which bears most forcefully on Britain's defence priorities. I leave aside the political wisdom of a 'Fortress Falklands' policy and whether the liberty of those we are supposed to be sustaining within an isolated armed camp has proper meaning. I refer solely to the huge cost of such a policy, its impact on defence spending, and the consequences it has for the deployment of large numbers of our air, land and sea forces.

The two foundations of Britain's commitment to NATO—its support for the British Army on the Rhine, and the maintenance of a substantial surface fleet—are being put in jeopardy, at the very time they should be strengthened, in order to make a conventional response to threatened Soviet aggression more credible, and thus raise the nuclear threshold.

The pursuit of the 'Fortress Falklands' policy is officially estimated to cost £1,860 million over three years—averaging about £600 million a year. Unofficial estimates put the real cost at more than £3 million a day. And although such costs could be reduced in later years, the enormous and disproportionate burden on the Royal Navy will remain.

More than a quarter of the Navy's entire destroyer and frigate fleet is committed to the Falklands, either on patrol or in transit to and from station. And that represents up to half the Navy's modern ships.

This weakening of NATO's northern flank could not have been more dramatically illustrated than by the huge Soviet Naval exercises of April 1984. NATO chiefs were clearly startled by the speed and size of the Soviet operation.

Yet Mrs Thatcher has been reported as saying that the Falklands garrison would remain 'for a thousand years, if necessary'. For my part, I fear that in the meantime the defence of Western Europe could be sacrificed to that vainglorious obsession.

The second distorting factor—and seemingly no less of an obsession—is the Trident missile programme. By any standards this represents a serious and unilateral escalation of nuclear weaponry by Britain—and an incitement to nuclear proliferation by every other would-be nuclear power in the world. It does nothing to enhance our authority when we should be pushing for controls on the spread of nuclear technology and seeking agreement on nuclear arms reductions. Quite the reverse. Indeed, I believe it will do nothing to increase our security. Nor will it improve the prospects of a lasting peace, particularly when the British government firmly refuses to include Polaris, and by implication its successor, Trident, in the Geneva talks.

Of course, Liberals have always opposed the concept of an independent nuclear deterrent. I have always considered that it must be either surplus to collective Western requirements, or useless when challenged independently. I have never found convincing the argument that 'tearing off the arm' of the Soviet bear would be a comforting thought if at the same time it precipitated national suicide. Nor do I agree with the Prime Minister that its possession is of use in deterring a conventional attack by a non-nuclear adversary. The Argentine invasion of the Falklands was evidence enough of that.

There are in any case growing doubts about how 'independent' the Trident system would be with the rockets based in Georgia for refitting. But it is the cost of this grand delusion—officially now nearly £10 billion and rising daily—which has united the majority of the country, including many in the armed forces, in opposition to the project. In the words of the House of Commons Select Committee on Defence: 'It is very difficult to see how it will be possible to give top priority to the Trident programme . . . without something else being squeezed out.'

It is Trident which must be squeezed out—and soon, before the annual costs rise to £1 billion and more from 1988 onwards. If its cancellation were combined with a determination to emerge from the blind alley of 'Fortress Falklands', proper defence priorities, with a greater emphasis on non-nuclear defence, could then be developed. And the scrapping of Trident could provide Britain with an opportunity to help break the nuclear arms deadlock.

The greatest danger to world security still lies in the arms race between the superpowers.

I have been disappointed at the government's approach to the whole Geneva process during the Conservatives' five or six years in office. I write as one who has always been, and remains, a believer in multilateral disarmament. But I fear that this process has given multilateral disarmament a bad name. We have ended up with Cruise and Pershing missiles deployed in Western Europe. We shall end up with SS21s, 22s and 23s brought into Czechoslovakia and East Germany. Instead of moving towards multilateral disarmament, we have managed to achieve multilateral further armament. There has been a ratcheting up process in the last five years. The time has come to start operating the ratchet down.

What is the proper way for Britain and the West to address the question of relationships with the Soviet Union, and the process of disarmament?

We should pay attention to words recently addressed to us by church leaders in Scotland. They rightly pointed out that the increased sophistication and power of this weaponry does not increase security. The word 'security' is bandied about in a reckless way. In true terms, they say, such weapons increase the world's insecurity, and they are right to point out:

> 'We appear to be locked into an unalterable assumption that the hostility between the superpowers will continue indefinitely. We are planning for a twenty-first century which will be characterised by the same unresolved confrontation.'

Now that confrontation is spreading from the earth to the heavens above us.

We must not continue on that assumption. We should not assume permanent confrontation nor believe that the only way to achieve so-called security is to spend more and more on bigger and better arms, or even more expensive technological methods to try to make those arms inoperative.

The breakdown in the Geneva talks on Intermediate

Nuclear Forces and the Soviet walk-out was both tragic and avoidable. The differences between the two superpowers were comparatively small—insignificantly so when the margin of dispute is compared with the huge stocks of overkill possessed by both sides. That gap of 390 warheads amounted to less than one per cent of total existing arsenals.

Now the disarmament process is under way again, but I fear the omens will not be good unless both West and East approach negotiations in a different spirit. There must be a political will to find a common cause: that cause is surely what the Palme Report called common security. There is now a broad balance of destructive capacity between the superpowers. What is required is a definition of advantage which does not depend on trying to find superiority, offensive or defensive, over the other side but rests instead on the great economic and social benefits to the citizens of the whole world if the process of armament could be first contained and then put into reverse.

I have long been in favour of a nuclear freeze for precisely that reason. It provides a context of security which breeds confidence and makes it easier to start on disarmament proper. Star Wars, the Strategic Defence Initiative, by contrast is profoundly insecure: ostensibly pacific in purpose but in practice, like the ABM before it, condemning the world to decades of dangerous instability, as thousands of billions of dollars are lavished on a technological game of hide-and-seek, with levels of mistrust between the superpowers institutionalised into the next century.

Star Wars are not in the interests of Britain or Europe from a military and strategic standpoint, but they are even more dangerous to the whole world in their destabilisation of deterrence. I have been disappointed that by its approval of research on SDI the British government may have given our American allies the impression that we will support deployment.

It is small wonder that the Soviet Union, which is relatively backward in technology, puts this issue near the top of the agenda in Geneva. Their concern at the project was made very plain to me on my visit to the Soviet Union in 1984. These, and other contentious matters, can only be discussed successfully in a constructive atmosphere. Britain should contribute to that by making it plain that she will include her so-called independent deterrent in the talks and by accepting that goodwill on both sides is essential, rather than by the constant claim that without the blunt assertion of force, in deploying Cruise and Pershing, the Russians would not have come crawling back to the negotiating table. Britain can also help by making its commitment to a NATO conventional response strategy more palpable, by cancelling Trident and equipping its armed forces properly.

It is my contention that arms control is not mechanistic, depending on hardware counts, but political, depending on the creation of decent relationships between the adversaries.

Détente between East and West creates a climate in which important contacts can be established and productive dialogue can take place. It has a direct bearing on human happiness. For example, there is a close correlation between the breakdown of détente and the Soviet clampdown on immigration permits issued to Jews wishing to move to Israel, or dissidents wanting to emigrate. It also has a direct effect on our economies. Western contracts for the Siberian gas pipeline project would have gone ahead unchallenged, creating many jobs in the process, if the political climate between East and West had been better.

That is why I applauded the initiative of Pierre Trudeau in seeking a five-power Nuclear Summit. The former Canadian Liberal Prime Minister—whose contribution to world politics will be sorely missed—spoke of how deeply troubled he was

'by an intellectual climate of acrimony and uncertainty; by the parlous state of East/West relations; by a superpower relationship which is dangerously confrontational, and by a

widening gap between military strategy and
political purpose. All these reveal most
profoundly the urgent need to assert the
pre-eminence of the mind of man over the
machines of war.'

Europe has a major role to play. Both our geographical
position between the two superpowers and our extensive
links with the countries of the developing world put Europe
in a unique position to press for détente and disarmament.

I look forward to the day when, through Europe, we can
play the role of honest broker in world affairs. Mrs Thatcher's government and its allies the Reaganites have not made
the world a safer or better place. They have done nothing to
solve the problems of the Middle East, which remains a
highly dangerous flashpoint of world tension. With their
money and political support they have in many parts of the
world backed the wrong people. If we value liberal
democracy, which is a diminishing commodity in the world
today, we must strongly resist totalitarian tendencies of
both the left and the right. We do not assist the process by
supporting everyone in Latin America who happens to be
anti-communist. The position of the present American
administration—and indeed of our own government, in
resuming arms sales to Chile—played into the hands of the
Marxists who are then unable to distinguish between liberal
democracies and fascist dictatorships or military regimes.

The real enemy in Latin America, as in many areas of the
developing world, is not communism but injustice and
poverty. As Robert McNamara put it a decade ago:

'One third of mankind today lives in an
environment of relative abundance. But two
thirds of mankind—more than 2,000 million
individuals—remain entrapped in a cruel web
of circumstances that severely limits their right
to the necessities of life. They are caught in
the grip of hunger and malnutrition; high

138

illiteracy and inadequate education; shrinking opportunity and corrosive poverty. The gap between rich and poor nations is no longer merely a gap. It is a chasm.'

The Brandt Report, stressing the economic strength of the North, possessing over ninety per cent of the world's manufacturing industry, illustrates that divide in more detail:

'The North including Eastern Europe has a quarter of the world's population and four fifths of its income; the South, including China, has three billion people—three quarters of the world's population but living on one fifth of the world's income. In the North, the average person can expect to live for more than seventy years; he or she will rarely be hungry, and will be educated at least up to secondary level. In the countries of the South the great majority of people have a life expectancy of closer to fifty years; in the poorest countries one out of every four children dies before the age of five; one fifth or more of all the people in the South suffer from hunger and malnutrition; fifty per cent have no chance to become literate.'

The awful scenes of famine in Ethiopia witnessed on our television screens in the winter of 1984 demonstrated this all too vividly. The reaction of the British public to that famine was one of tremendous concern and generosity. But we must learn the lessons of Ethiopia; in future, we must ensure the direction of sufficient aid to similarly endangered areas in good time to prevent such disasters occurring.

Another illustration of the huge difference between North and South is to put it in terms of our daily existence and to contrast the carefree attitude that advanced nations have to precious resources and supplies of energy.

Barbara Ward and Rene Dubois, writing in *Only One Earth* contrasted the *waste* with the *need* when they wrote:

> 'Items junked each year in the USA include 48 billion metal cans, 26 billion glass bottles, 65 billion metal bottle caps and 7 billion cars . . . an average North American baby is likely to use up the world's energy supplies 500 times faster than the average baby born in the Third World.'

Such frightening figures almost pass beyond the limits of our comprehension. If we were personally to witness a fraction of the suffering and degradation which lie behind these statistics, the horror of what is happening would strike deep into our souls. Television news reports allow us to become anaesthetised to pain—yet even the glimpses of that reality we see in the comfort of our homes convey something of the immeasurable scale of the problem, inducing feelings for some of helplessness, anger, and perhaps shame. Others will see the future dangers of such an imbalance.

The linkage between a hungry and divided world and peace and security should be obvious. Self-interest alone should drive the rich industrialised nations of the North to realise that these cries of distress they hear from hundreds of millions, wracked by starvation and disease, are a chilling warning of what might be the ultimate political explosion. Such retribution would be a bitter legacy for future generations.

As the Brandt Report itself emphasises: 'More arms do not make mankind safer, only poorer.' Arms consume an obscene amount of our world resources. As Barbara Ward told the UN Habitat Conference in 1976:

> 'It is simply not possible to underline sufficiently the appalling state of a collective imagination when 300 billion dollars for arms seems normal but 3 billion dollars for water exceptional.'

Willy Brandt, in the introduction to his report, made the same point with different illustrations. Brandt put the annual military bill at almost $450 billion. Official development aid, he pointed out, amounted to less than five per cent of that figure.

So what is the response of the West—and Britain in particular—to the two challenges of world poverty and nuclear rivalry?

With the remarkable exception of the Ethiopian famine, I am sorry to say that Britain has been turning in on itself, and away from the outside world, in recent years. It has been part of our overall loss of self-confidence to see foreigners as unfriendly, overseas competitors as a threat, international obligations as infringing our sovereignty. Tighter and tighter restrictions on immigration, rising support for import controls, higher and higher fees imposed on overseas students, fantasies about the Common Market—these are all part of the same mood, the same welling up of nationalism and xenophobia.

The Conservative government's negative response to the Brandt Report—reasserting its faith in the market economy, and its concern to reduce public expenditure—hardly begins to address the issues it raised.

There is a generation in Britain today deeply worried by the practice of world leaders of conducting their arguments at arms length, in an atmosphere of mutual hostility and personal ignorance. There is a crying need to give fresh impetus against the scandalous waste of human resources devoted to the arms race on both sides of the Iron Curtain.

The self-interest of the North is bound up with the future of the South. Cutting aid is no way to help the world economy out of recession. The idea that we can somehow opt out of the awkward problems of North–South relations, cut back savagely on our aid programme, close down much of our efforts in education and training, does not bear examination. Of course we have to limit our efforts to our resources—but our resources are not as limited as the government seems to suggest. Of course we cannot bear the whole burden on our own—but neither this government nor the last has done much to pursue the possibilities for extending international co-operation.

The momentum of the West is entirely in the wrong direction—and reversing that retreat from world order and justice is a challenging and very great task.

Britain has a unique role to play, both in its membership of the European Community and in its still valuable links with developing nations through the Commonwealth. As a leading member of NATO, Britain could also play a vital role in pushing forward the cause of genuine nuclear disarmament and weapon control.

It has become far too fashionable in Britain and in the United States to denigrate the United Nations as a useless organisation. The smaller states in the world are vulnerable to internal overthrow, to neighbouring regimes, to other states and to the influences of big business. They are entitled to greater protection from some sort of international policeman. Instead of undermining the United Nations' authority, we should develop an active and positive role for that international organisation.

The Commonwealth has also been the victim of unjustified criticism. The first generation of Commonwealth leaders, with all their ambivalence—but also fascination—about Britain, have mostly gone. Their successors are more disillusioned, but also more realistic about the value of cultural links, of communication and of economic ties.

Britain's position as leader of a Commonwealth with forty-nine member countries (almost one third of the UN's membership, including a high proportion of its smallest and poorest members) has tremendous potential. It is valuable above all as a network of communication across the globe, which cuts across regional groupings and political ties. It does not fit into any black and white view of the world, in which each nation must choose between the Champion of Western Values and the Evil Empire; but that is precisely its value, in providing flexible and informal links which educate and inform all the participants.

A British government which wishes to wash its hands of the Third World, of the problems of poverty, famine and economic development, will have little use for the Commonwealth. A government which sees the global chequerboard as one with only two serious players will have little use for it either; Grenada can be left to be freed from Soviet dominance by the American marines, the Southern African states can be left to choose between the hegemony of South Africa and the unfriendly hands of the USSR. But a government which wants to help small states protect their independence from the superpowers, to assist their political and economic development, will find the Commonwealth invaluable as a channel of discreet influence and advice—in both directions.

Above all, we cannot cut Britain off from the rest of the world, nor can we sever the bonds of a common humanity which link us all. I am not ashamed of being an internationalist. I *am* ashamed to see so many signs of chauvinism, of mean-mindedness towards foreigners, of resentment at the ties of international co-operation in Britain.

A hundred years ago, with a British Army attempting to subdue Afghanistan, William Gladstone made a classic statement of internationalism when he said:

'Remember the rights of the savage, as we call him. Remember the happiness of his humble home, remember that the sanctity of life in the hill villages of Afghanistan among the winter snows is as inviolable in the eyes of Almighty God as can be your own. Remember that He who has united you together as human beings in the same flesh and blood has bound you by the law of mutual love; that that mutual love is not limited by the shores of this island, is not limited by the boundaries of Christian civilisation; that it passes over the whole surface of the earth, and embraces the meanest along with the greatest in its unmeasured scope.'

David Steel

Epilogue

In his address to both Houses of Congress in 1952, Winston Churchill declared: 'Our complicated society would be deeply injured if we did not practise what is called in the United States the bi-partisan habit of mind.' His words found an echo more recently in Lord Stockton's eloquent demand for a 'national approach' to Britain's problems.

Both these former Prime Ministers presided over Britain's fortunes in the age before the Conservative and Labour parties had both deserted the field of consensus. One cannot imagine that Mrs Thatcher, whose very claim to fame is that she has abandoned such an approach *inside* her own party— let alone towards other parties—would find this appealing. The Labour Party has over the same six years deserted many of its traditional voters with a dash to the militant left. Amongst Labour activists the very words 'bipartisan', 'national' or 'consensus' are anathema.

Yet I believe that what is required desperately in our country today is a national lead which will elicit a positive response from the greatest possible number of our fellow citizens, in short to find what Trevor Phillips calls a new consensus.

Such a view is wrongly dismissed by the hard ideologists of right and left as a search for the lowest common denominator, the soggy centre.

That is not our aim. It is easy to fight the class war. It is far more difficult but more worthwhile to act as the catalyst of new policies and attitudes, which could bring unity where there is division. In this book we have attempted to outline policies—and more importantly, values—which will take us in a new direction, towards a partnership society.

The paradox of modern Britain is that we need more diversity *and* more unity. The schizophrenia of 'Two Nations' has served us very badly. It gives the impression that the only choice each of us has is to decide which 'side' he or she is on in the battle between left and right, worker and manager, Labour and Tory. This is too simplistic. It distorts human nature and it has deformed our life together in this country. If we could accept the challenge of pluralism, of welcoming people and communities in all their glorious difference and individuality, providing ways that they can come together freely in co-operative partnership, we would find it easier to recapture what unites us as a nation.

This book has not been an attempt to write a comprehensive manifesto. Its purpose is to stimulate debate on the directions a Liberal and Alliance programme might take at an election in the late 1980s. I believe we shall have an historic opportunity then for a confident reassertion of Britain's capacity to solve deep problems and conquer engrained prejudices by engaging in a process of adventurous political and social experiment. By the year 2000 A.D. we can have built a partnership society which provides greater self-fulfilment and satisfaction for its individual members and a greater sense of success for the country as a whole.

Certain themes have constantly re-emerged in our different contributions to this analysis. By dispersing power and responsibility you tap new resources of energy and commitment: this idea finds common expression in Ralf Dahrendorf's thoughts on the Welfare State and Richard Holme's plea for fundamental constitutional reform.

I was very struck by Prince Charles's speech to the Institute of Directors in February when he called for greater community enterprise. He talked of 'the immense human potential and resource waiting to be given the incentive and encouragement to play a fuller part in contributing to the common good'.

That community involvement, as John Alderson points out, has important social effects. Instead of the police supervising local people and being perceived and resented as agents of the State, they could become welcome and accepted members of a local team working for the good of a community that everyone valued.

Economically, too, greater local initiative, a regeneration of the economy from the grass roots up, is, as Nancy Seear has pointed out, one of the ways of providing work and a recovery of self-respect for thousands of people, whose lives are leaking away in a morass of uselessness.

Partnership has many local applications but it is also relevant to the strategic direction of the economy, which is essential in an economy as run down as ours but which has been sadly neglected by the Conservative government. James Meade's analysis rests precisely on a partnership between government, employer and employee in a search for a new synthesis between success and fairness. Derek Ezra shows how government and large companies could, by enlightened self-interest, build a partnership with the smaller companies with whom they deal to build up their strength and expertise, with benefit to the whole economy.

Competition alone is not enough—and the answer cannot be State collectivism. I am convinced that we are on the right lines in searching for ways to express the ideas of working together and sharing in success, which are as natural as breathing to British people, but which have been made impossible by our institutions and official attitudes.

I believe we are working with the grain of the British genius, rather than against it like the ideologists. We have to work to change popular values and expectations. We have to look to the future and thus help to restore the sense of hope and purpose, which is sadly lacking in our country today.

We must not be afraid of an element of vitality and excitement which has gone out of so many people's lives. A tired country is also a frightened country, and a sign of that fear is resistance to new ideas and a clinging to outworn ones.

In my first speech as Liberal leader I said:

> 'I look forward and I see a country of co-operation, not class war; of liberty, not bureaucracy; of power dispersed, not centralised; of compassion, not indifference; of openness and candour, not secrecy and evasion.
>
> I look ahead and I see a Britain of high standards, not shoddiness; prosperous, not depressed; with achievements to its credit, not failure.
>
> I see a society that is prudent in its use of resources, not profligate; in harmony with the natural world, not at war with it; respectful of all citizens, not contemptuous of them.
>
> I see a nation with an honoured place in the community of nations, not for the tattered remnants of its imperial or industrial might, but for the quality of its civilisation.'

I hope some of the ideas in this book will point us in that direction.